Pagan
'
Shaman l
...*an ever-growing librar*

Moon Books has created two unique series where leading authors and practitioners come together to share their knowledge, passion and expertise across the complete Pagan spectrum. If you would like to contribute to either series, our proposal procedure is simple and quick, just visit our website (www.MoonBooks.net) and click on Author Inquiry to begin the process.

If you are a reader with a comment about a book or a suggestion for a title we'd love to hear from you! You can find us at facebook.com/MoonBooks or you can keep up to date with new releases etc on our dedicated Portals page at facebook.com/pagan-portalsandshamanpathways/

'Moon Books has achieved that rare feat of being synonymous with top-quality authorship AND being endlessly innovative and exciting.'
Kate Large, Pagan Dawn

Pagan Portals

Animal Magic, Rachel Patterson
An introduction to the world of animal magic and working with animal spirit guides

Australian Druidry, Julie Brett
Connect with the magic of the southern land, its seasons, animals, plants and spirits

Gods and Goddesses of Ireland,
Meet the Gods and Goddesses of Pagan Ireland in myth and modern practice

Grimalkyn: The Witch's Cat, Martha Gray
A mystical insight into the cat as a power animal

Hedge Riding, Harmonia Saille
The hedge is the symbolic boundary between the two worlds and this book will teach you how to cross that hedge

Hedge Witchcraft, Harmonia Saille
Learning by experiencing is about trusting your instincts and connecting with your inner spirit

Hekate, Vivienne Moss
The Goddess of Witches, Queen of Shades and Shadows, and the ever-eternal Dark Muse haunts the pages of this poetic devotional, enchanting those who love Her with the charm only this Dark Goddess can bring

Herbs of the Sun, Moon and Planets, Steve Andrews
The planets that rule over herbs that grow on Earth

Hoodoo, Rachel Patterson
Learn about and experience the fascinating magical art of Hoodoo

Irish Paganism, Morgan Daimler
Reconstructing the beliefs and practices of pre-Christian Irish Paganism for the modern world

Kitchen Witchcraft, Rachel Patterson
Take a glimpse at the workings of a Kitchen Witch and share in the crafts

Meditation, Rachel Patterson
An introduction to the beautiful world of meditation

Merlin: Once and Future Wizard, Elen Sentier
Merlin in history, Merlin in mythology, Merlin through the ages
and his continuing relevance

Moon Magic, Rachel Patterson
An introduction to working with the phases of the Moon

Nature Mystics, Rebecca Beattie
Tracing the literary origins of modern Paganism

Pan, Mélusine Draco
An historical, mythological and magical insight into the God Pan

Pathworking through Poetry, Fiona Tinker
Discover the esoteric knowledge in the works of Yeats, O'Sullivan
and other poets

Runes, Kylie Holmes
The Runes are a set of 24 symbols that are steeped in history,
myths and legends. This book offers practical and accessible information for anyone to understand this ancient form of divination

Sacred Sex and Magick, Web PATH Center
Wrap up ecstasy in love to create powerful magick, spells and
healing

Spirituality without Structure, Nimue Brown
The only meaningful spiritual journey is the one you consciously
undertake

The Awen Alone, Joanna van der Hoeven
An introductory guide for the solitary Druid

The Cailleach, Rachel Patterson
Goddess of the ancestors, wisdom that comes with age, the
weather, time, shape-shifting and winter

The Morrigan, Morgan Daimler
On shadowed wings and in raven's call, meet the ancient Irish
Goddess of war, battle, prophecy, death, sovereignty, and magic

Urban Ovate, Brendan Howlin
Simple, accessible techniques to bring Druidry to the wider public

Your Faery Magic, Halo Quin
Tap into your Natural Magic and become the Fey you are

Zen Druidry, Joanna van der Hoeven
Zen teachings and Druidry combine to create a peaceful life path
that is completely dedicated to the here and now

Shaman Pathways

Aubry's Dog, Melusine Draco
A practical and essential guide to using canine magical energies

Black Horse White Horse, Mélusine Draco
Feel the power and freedom as *Black Horse, White Horse* guides
you down the magical path of this most noble animal

Celtic Chakras, Elen Sentier
Tread the British native shaman's path, explore the Goddess
hidden in the ancient stories; walk the Celtic chakra spiral
labyrinth

Druid Shaman, Danu Forest
A practical guide to Celtic shamanism with exercises and
techniques as well as traditional lore for exploring the Celtic
Otherworld

Elen of the Ways, Elen Sentier
British shamanism has largely been forgotten: the reindeer
Goddess of the ancient Boreal forest is shrouded in
mystery...follow her deer-trods to rediscover her old ways

Following the Deer Trods, Elen Sentier
A practical handbook for anyone wanting to begin the old British
paths. Follows on from *Elen of the Ways*

Trees of the Goddess, Elen Sentier
Work with the trees of the Goddess and the old ways of Britain

Way of the Faery Shaman, Flavia Kate Peters
Your practical insight into Faeries and the elements they engage to
unlock real magic that is waiting to help you

Web of Life, Yvonne Ryves
A new approach to using ancient ways in these contemporary and
often challenging times to weave your life path

The Crane Bag

Storytelling and practicality combine to guide the reader through the creation and uses of ritual tools. Joanna is clearly inspired by the ancient tales and offers useful insights and ethical understanding to ground old teachings in a contemporary setting. A clear passion for the Land permeates the book and will inspire many readers to deepen their links to their own local landscapes. The ritual format moves beyond the Wiccan styles familiar in so many other books, to consider practices rooted in myth and Insular Celtic culture. Whilst built on solid scholarship, this book is accessibly written and engaging – a definite bonus to the bookshelves of those starting out in Druidry as well as experienced walkers wanting to revise and reconsider their journeys.

Robin Herne, Course Leader for the Honours Degree in Religious Studies and Ethics, University Campus Suffolk and author of *Old Gods, New Druids, Bard Song* and *A Dangerous Place*.

Concise, precise and, despite its brevity, comprehensive. Indeed, just like a true crane bag, this book contains all you need plus that little bit extra. Its open and friendly style makes it an easy read and it gets directly to the point. But don't be deceived by that into thinking it is superficial. Far from it. A wonderful little tome that provides the perfect start for a lifelong practical exploration of an essential part of the Druid Way.

Graeme K Talboys, author of *The Path Through the Forest: A Druid Guidebook, Way of the Druid* and *Arianrhod's Dance*

Pagan Portals – The Crane Bag is a nice little introduction to a very English style of 'Druidry' (Druidism), which is in essence nature worship. In it the author shares her passion for the land and shows how to do simple rituals upon it. She also shares ways to cultivate respect for the Earth and all her creatures. Like Joanna I always do my Druid rites out of doors and in this book I find a kindred spirit.

Ellen Evert Hopman, author of *A Legacy of Druids*

Pagan Portals

The Crane Bag

A Druid's Guide to Ritual Tools
and Practices

Pagan Portals
The Crane Bag

A Druid's Guide to Ritual Tools
and Practices

Joanna van der Hoeven

Winchester, UK
Washington, USA

First published by Moon Books, 2017
Moon Books is an imprint of John Hunt Publishing Ltd., Laurel House, Station Approach,
Alresford, Hants, SO24 9JH, UK
office1@jhpbooks.net
www.johnhuntpublishing.com
www.moon-books.net

For distributor details and how to order please visit the 'Ordering' section on our website.

Text copyright: Joanna van der Hoeven 2016

ISBN: 978 1 78535 573 8
978 1 78535 574 5 (ebook)
Library of Congress Control Number:

A CIP catalogue record for this book is available from the British Library.

Design: Stuart Davies

Printed and bound by CPI Group (UK) Ltd, Croydon, CR0 4YY, UK

We operate a distinctive and ethical publishing philosophy in all
areas of our business, from our global network of authors to
production and worldwide distribution.

CONTENTS

Acknowledgements

My thanks to Aurora Stone, for her watchful eye and for all her support.

A special thank you to Yannick Dubois, whose artwork among these pages is pure awen.

www.yannickdubois.com

Introduction

This book is a guide on the ritual tools and practices found in the Druid tradition. As part of the Pagan Portals series, it is intended as a brief introduction to the subject, allowing the reader to further develop their own path in their own time and in their own fashion.

The crane bag is a wonderful theme in Celtic mythology, found mostly in the tales of the poet-warrior Fionn Mac Cumhail, who inherited the crane bag from his father. This bag held the special treasures of the land and was made from the skin of a crane who was, in actuality, a woman enchanted into crane form. We can view the myths that surround the crane bag as those of the gifts of sovereignty, bestowed by the goddess upon worthy heroes as is typical of Celtic mythology. The goddess held great abundance and gifts within her womb, and only those who passed the test and were deemed fit were able to be gifted with this most precious treasure. As the bestower of sovereignty, the goddess fades and emerges time and again within the old stories, as does the crane bag, appearing and disappearing from myth when there is need. The sea god, Manannan, is the original owner of the crane bag and through his love for the goddess gives and takes it back throughout the telling of the tales.

Within the mythology of the crane bag, those who follow the Celtic Druid tradition can come to know a very beneficial tool in their learning, the gifts of which are endless. Within the crane bag are not only the tools of the Druid, but also a symbolism of the gift of the goddess, of sovereignty. With the proper use, it can further the Druid in working with the tides of nature, finding their proper place in the grand scheme of things, living in balance, harmony and peace. In ritual use, these tools can guide the Druid to deeper levels of meaning and understanding within the tradition, helping the Druid on her journey throughout life towards integration in a holistic way of being in the world.

We will not only look at the ritual tools of the Druid, but also the practices enacted within ritual that help the seeker of the way to find that connection, be it with the ancestors, the gods, the spirits of place or the Otherworld. Combined with the tools of the Druid's craft held within the crane bag, we can learn how to walk the path of the Druid with honour and respect.

May your path be enchanted with the old tales and the songs of the land!

Chapter One

What is the Crane Bag?

Three rejoicings followed by sorrow: a wooer's, a thief's, a tale-bearer's.
Irish triad

The Story of How the Crane Bag Came to Be

Aoife, daughter of Dealbhaoth, was one of the most beautiful young ladies in the land. She had hair that shone like pure gold in the sun, eyes as blue as the sea and skin as pale as fresh milk. Upon her face there was no blemish, and upon her lips no unkind word was ever spoken. She was tall and strong, graceful and generous.

Iuchra, daughter of Abhartach, was also very beautiful. She had long dark hair like a raven's wing, and lips as red as cherries. Her eyes were the green of leaves in the flush of first spring, her form willowy and light, and her laughter was like a stream tumbling over water. But her laughter grew less and less, as she came to know Aoife, and a jealousy grew in her heart. Lovely though Iuchra was, she thought that she was lessened when compared to Aoife's beauty. And so a dark seed was born within her heart.

One day, as the young women went down to the meadows to collect herbs and flowers, they came across a young man upon a red roan mare who had lost his way. His name was Ilbhreac, and his dark hair curled about his forehead, his smile lit up the sky. As he approached the two women, they both could not help but fall in love with his beauty. His voice was as sweet as honey, and his face bore no ill will or deceit. He shone with a radiance of pure honesty.

'Tell me, fair maidens, the name of the nearest village? I fear that I have lost my way,' he said.

'You are very near to Maith Geal,' said Iuchra, looking at him from beneath her long lashes. ''Tis but half a mile to the south,' she said, extending her arm in the direction of the village. She smiled her best smile at him. 'You're most welcome to come by for refreshment,' she said, in the hopes that she herself could bear him a cup of their sweetest mead.

But Ilbhreac had only eyes for Aoife, who smiled and patted the neck of his horse as the mare nuzzled against her shoulder. 'And are you both from that village?' Ilbhreac asked Aoife.

'Yes,' Aoife replied. 'You look like you have travelled a long way, and we can also provide refreshment for your horse.'

'Thank you, that would be most kind,' the young man said. 'I am with the Fianna, and have been sent out to get to know the lay of the land, having recently joined their band of warriors and protectors.' At the mention of the famed band of heroes that kept the land free from raiders, the eyes of both maidens widened. Here was a man of courage and daring. Ilbhreac smiled at them once again, and disembarked from his mount, walking on foot with the two women back towards the village.

He was received with the traditional hospitality, and spent the night within the village rath. Songs and stories were told around the fire, and Iuchra managed to sit at Ilbhreac's right hand, to fill his cup with mead and hopefully garner his affection. Still Ilbhreac only had eyes for Aoife, however, and when she was asked to sing his heart was lost completely. Iuchra saw this, and a hatred for the fair maiden grew within her breast until it flamed upon her cheeks and set her eyes alight. She knew what she would do.

The next day, as Ilbhreac left them, promising to return within the fortnight, Iuchra turned to Aoife. 'Let us go down to the waters,' she smiled sweetly, her honeyed words hiding the bitterness inside. 'It is warm enough to bathe by the lake today,' she said.

'Oh, yes, let's do that!' Aoife said, clapping her hands together and smiling her beautiful smile. She hugged Iuchra and grabbed her hand, running with her down to the shore of the lake. 'Last one in has to milk the kicking cow!' she said, laughing as she stripped off her clothes and dived into the lake.

Iuchra watched as Aoife dove beneath the water, and then she raised her hands above her head. 'By the power of sun and moon, by the power of water and wave, by the power of blood and bone, by the power of wind and rain, may Aoife be turned into a crane!'

Aoife surfaced from the water, and looked questioningly towards the shore. 'Why are you not coming into the water?' she asked Iuchra.

Iuchra stood in her place and finished her chant. 'By the power of stone and sea, by the power of lightning and storm, by the power of these things I name, may Aoife be turned into a crane!'

Suddenly the clouds darkened overhead, and lightning flashed into the distance. 'Iuchra,' said Aoife softly. 'What have you done?'

But Iuchra did not answer. Instead, a flash of lightning hit the water where Aoife stood, half immersed in the cool, clear lake. Iuchra shielded her eyes from the blast, and when she turned back to see what had happened, a crane stood where Aoife had once stood, its long legs in the water, its pale wings flapping in surprise.

'Iuchra,' said the crane, its voice slowly changing from the melodious tone of Aoife to the harsh chittering and croak of the bird, 'how long must I remain in this form?'

'Two hundred years must you remain in bird form,' Iuchra shouted out her rage, 'and on to the lands of Manannan must you dwell, never to return here again!'

Aoife trièd to call out to Iuchra, but her throat would no longer give her human voice, and she could do nothing but chitter and cackle like a crane. She spread her wings in great sorrow, and flew out towards the sea, banished from her home by the power of Iuchra's spell.

For two hundred years, Aoife circled the lands of the sea god, Manannan. She wept inwardly at her plight, and stood vigil every sunset in the hopes that the spell might be broken. She often kept Manannan company in her bird form as he came to watch the golden disc sink down into his kingdom beneath the waves. He grew fond of her company, and often would reach out and stroke the long, graceful neck of the bird.

For two hundred years they kept each other company each day as the sun set, casting its light upon the water. As the sun set beneath the waves and two hundred years had passed, Manannan reached out to stroke the gentle bird's neck like he always did. But his hand reached out only to empty air. He turned to look to see what had befallen his friend, and there upon the shore laid a young woman, the fairest maiden he had ever seen. Her long golden hair lay across the rocks like a last ray of sunlight, and her alabaster skin shone in the last of the setting sun. His heart broke for her, and even as he watched she turned into an old woman, and then died as the last ray of sunlight touched her face before it sank beneath the waves.

'A dreadful magic has been enacted here,' Manannan said, picking up the body of Aoife. 'But from this beautiful companion shall arise that which can contain all the treasures of these lands. Long she bore her fate, long was her enchantment. Large was her heart to endure, so large that it shall hereto be that which all the treasures of mine are bestowed and kept safe therein.' Saying that, he turned her body into a leather bag, and the image of a crane with knotwork encompassing it was carved into its surface with great skill. 'This is the crane bag, and within it I shall place everything that is precious to me,' said Manannan.

Into the bag he placed his shirt and his dagger, along with a girdle made by the great blacksmith god Goibhne. A hook from that same god was also placed into the bag, along with the King of Scotland's shears and the helmet from the King of Lochlainn. Into the bag also went the carved bones of Asal's swine, and a girdle made from the great whale.

Manannan kept the crane bag close to his heart, and hung it about his neck so that it lay against his breast. When the time for a great hero was at hand, Manannan would bring him the crane bag, bestowing this great gift that held various treasures from various times of the land throughout the ages. Manannan would give this gift freely, filled with treasures old and new, and take it back again when it was time for a new hero to be born. He knew that these treasures would be kept safe, as in the womb of a great goddess, for he trusted in his long-time friend, the crane, and knew that she would keep these safe for all eternity even as she bore out her fate until the end of her days.

And what happened to Iuchra and Ilbhreac? Well, that is a tale for another day.

The Crane Bag as Soul Map

As we have seen in the story above, the crane bag carries the treasures of the land. These treasures began with Manannan and were later gifted to various heroes in Irish legend in turn. The crane bag held all that was precious to Manannan, and we can use this concept to create our own crane bag. What we place into the crane bag is a representation of who we are, with gifts from loved ones, fetishes we may have found on our travels, power objects and more.

In the Druid tradition, the crane bag also carries the tools of the trade, so to speak. Though there isn't a designated list of tools, per se, that all Druids use, there are a few that many agree upon in modern Druidry as being part of the tradition. You don't need to have these tools to be a Druid. However, they can be an important part of your tradition and help you to locate your place in the world.

When we have physical representations of concepts and ideas, they can become *more real* to us in our daily lives. The crane bag can be used to create a physical soul map that we can look at, study and rearrange as needed. What we place into the crane bag is that which represents us at this point in time. When we draw an item forth from the bag in ritual, we are using something tangible to express the spiritual. We can carry these items with us wherever we go, dependent upon the size of the crane bag, or we can use it solely for ritual use.

The crane bag can be perceived in a shamanistic sense, containing that which the Druid uses to walk between the worlds in ritual. We can compare it to the Native American medicine bag that healers use in their work. The crane bag is also an expression of the soul of the Druid, where physical objects represent aspects of the Druid's journey. It has a very real, physical use as well as a spiritual use. Used in ritual, the crane bag connects the physical with the spiritual, allowing us walk between the worlds.

Chapter Two

The Importance of Ritual

Meistr pob gwaith yw ymarfer. (The achievement of all work is practice.)
Welsh saying

What is Ritual?

Ritual consists of a prescribed set of words and actions within a particular context used to bring about a desired outcome. Druid ritual uses words and actions within the context of an earth-based tradition to connect with the landscape, the gods, the ancestors and so on. For the Druid, connection, relationship and integration with the landscape are at the heart of all that she does, whether in ritual or not. Ritual can be seen as a time set apart from daily life to reconnect the threads that bind us together with the land, with nature. We take a step back from what is perceived as the mundane and acknowledge the sacred. Ultimately, the Druid strives to perceive the sacred in everything, and ritual helps the Druid to achieve that vision.

Our modern lives are so busy, with work, family, media, technology and more. Ritual helps us to step back from the busyness, into another way of being. It is a change of consciousness, where we can shift our perception away from a singular view to a more plural view, integrating with the land around us, realising that we are a part of an ecosystem. Ritual is the act in the material world that connects us with a wider reality. It is an experience, not just a thought.

Ritual is that which helps us ground and centre in the present moment. When we stop, when we take a break to perform a ritual, we become aware of who, where and what we are at a particular point in time. We are rooted in the here and now, awake and aware to all that is happening around us. When we are awake, we are able to find our place in harmony with nature, finding a deep peace both within and without. It gives us an intention, a focus with which to work in the Druid tradition, to reweave the threads of connection.

Ritual also helps us to find stability. When we create rituals to perform repeatedly, we bring that sacred perspective more and more into our everyday life. These rituals needn't be identical each and every time; what is important is that the ritual is actually *done*. It is the experience of ritual that helps us to self-locate. We cannot do that simply by thinking about it; we must act as well. When we have acted out our rituals with some regularity, we may find that our connection to the natural world deepens. The ancient philosopher Lao Tzu once said:

Watch your thoughts, they become words;
watch your words, they become actions;
watch your actions, they become habits;
watch your habits, they become character;
watch your character, for it becomes your destiny.

We as humans are creatures of habit, and indeed these habits define us as people. A repeated action or behaviour will certainly have an impact on who we are as an individual. By using ritual we can break off from bad habits and thought patterns, for example, and find the sacredness within and all around us. It requires practice, as in the Welsh saying at the beginning of this chapter. We cannot just think about ritual; we must *do it*. If we take the time to reconnect with our place in the natural world, over and over again, then we will maintain that connection more and more throughout our lives until they are an example of pure integration and harmony.

Druid ritual is also a celebration. The eight seasonal festivals of modern Druidry help us to remember what is going on in nature at the present moment. There are many books that cover the eight seasonal festivals, their origins, meanings and ways to celebrate, and so we will not cover that here (see bibliography and suggested reading for more). Rather, we will look at how Druid ritual is set up, from start to finish, using our tools from the crane bag to find our soul map in our own environment.

Ritual is also a tool for transformation. When we have worked with intention and grounded ourselves in the present moment, we are transformed as our perception shifts from one perceived reality to another. Through the experience of ritual, we understand that our point of view is not the only one, and that perception shifts with intention. When we broaden our horizons, we cannot help but be transformed.

Re-enchanting the Soul

Work and familial obligations can sometimes weigh us down in a sea of mundane jobs, tasks, and commitments. With Druid ritual, we can re-enchant the soul to bring the magic back into our everyday lives, as we perceive the sacredness of all things. Then, we realise that there is no such thing as the mundane, only the sacred. The division between the two is realised as an illusion, and we are thus able to 'travel between the worlds'.

The Druid is always questing for inspiration, or *awen*. Awen is a Welsh word, sometimes translated as 'flowing spirit' or 'flowing inspiration'. Creativity is such a large part of the Druid path, where we are inspired and then inspire others in return. This exchange of inspiration is at the heart of all that we do, in deep relationship with the world around us. When we touch each other soul to soul, where we find intention blending together to work in harmony, then we are inspired. The Druid looks to the natural world around her to gain that inspiration. She takes her cues from nature as to how to live in the present moment, utterly awake and aware. So inspired, she lives her life as best she can as part of that environment, in tune with all that shares the same space. By doing so, she also inspires others in return.

Simply by getting outside and into 'nature', our awareness shifts. Though nature is something that we are a part of all the time, we often see it as something 'out there', as external to ourselves. When we realise that we are a part of nature, we shift from a self-centred perspective to an integrated one, thereby opening our eyes to the beauty and wonder that lies all around us each and every day. Taking a walk helps us to see the beauty of an oak tree in full leaf, to feel the warm caress of the summer wind, to feel the blessing of the rain or the exhilaration of a snowstorm. We awaken our senses to the world around us simply by being out in it, in nature, away from central heating and electricity, away from cars, phones and computers. Though all these things can be of great benefit, when we re-attune our senses to our 'natural' environment, we can also reawaken something that has long lain dormant within our souls. We can re-enchant our lives, re-wilding our souls. We can return to the very roots of our being. We can find the child-like wonder while looking at an ants' nest, or listening to the blackbird at dusk. We no longer become bored or jaded, but rather totally awake to the world around us. Our lives benefit from this re-enchantment on every level. This is the awen.

This is also the importance of ritual. When we take the time to re-enchant our souls, we make our lives more magical, more meaningful and more present. We can step outside the realm of 9-5 living. We enter into a state of intention and enchantment, inspired and inspiring others in return. In this, we find true relationship.

Chapter Three

The Druid's Tools

You've got to do your own growing, no matter how tall your father was.
Irish saying

It may sound odd to say so in a book like this, but in actuality a Druid doesn't need any tools at all. What matters most in ritual is the intention. A Druid can work with nothing more than his mind, if necessary. That said, tools can help us to focus that intention more clearly, and assist us in ritual simply by being physically present. If the tool is made by the Druid herself, then it becomes imbued with even more meaning. You can transport your tools to various locations by making your own crane bag.

The crane bag can be a simple cloth bag, cut from a basic circular pattern and tied with a drawstring top. It can be of any style or shape, and made from any material that is pleasing to you. Please ensure that if you are using leather that it has been ethically sourced. You can always buy a bag to use as your crane bag, if you wish, and there are many Pagan and occult suppliers that can make one to order, so that you can even have a crane design somewhere on the bag. There are also plenty of bags to be found in second-hand and charity shops, which can be painted and enhanced with your own skills and artistic ability. If you intend to carry your tools around with you in your crane bag, you will have to ensure that you have a bag large enough for the task.

I won't determine for you whether a handmade tool is better than a tool that is bought from a shop. Only you can decide that for yourself. What matters most is that it resonates with you. As Druidry is an earth-based tradition with a deep reverence for nature, what I would say is that it is important to ensure that your tools are as ethically sourced as possible. We must be aware of stones and crystals that are blasted from mountainsides, animals that may have suffered, or items produced in sweatshop factories. If you intend to do a peace ritual, for example, with a drinking horn from a cow who suffered from intensive farming, wearing robes made by a 12-year old girl in India working 16 hour days, then it is more than likely that the ritual will be entirely superficial. We must sacrifice any ignorance about what we use each and every day, as well as in ritual, in order to truly follow a religion or spirituality that has reverence for nature at its very heart.

Care for your tools is important as well. They should be kept in good condition. Be aware of how your tools react out of doors. A drum (with an ethically sourced skin, or a synthetic skin) will suffer in a damp or humid environment. A drum can equally be damaged by leaving it in a hot car, for instance. Metal can rust. Robes should, ideally, be practical, and not trip you up, causing you to fall into the fire.

When you first make or obtain your tools, you might like to sain (bless), smudge or consecrate them. This is essentially setting these tools apart from everyday use. However, it isn't necessary, and indeed some tools might be used in everyday life as well as in ritual. My Druid staff is a hazel walking stick, supporting me on my hikes through these lands and also used in ritual. It also has the benefit of being inconspicuous: I won't get odd looks walking down the high street with my walking stick and yet I can take this tool with me wherever I go.

To sain, smudge or consecrate a tool, you can use smoke (passing the tool through the curling wisps), sprinkle it with water, bury it in the earth, let it sit out in the full sun or moonlight. It is entirely up to you how you would like to dedicate this item to your practice. Simply let common sense prevail, as you don't want to ruin your item: don't dunk your drum in a sacred spring, for example.

What follows is a list of tools that Druids use today in their ritual practice. Some may only use one or two items from the list, some none at all, but essentially these are the tools that are associated with the tradition. You may find that you have other tools that you use outside this list, and this is perfectly fine. What matters most is the work that you do, and the intention that you set.

The Silver Branch

The silver branch features in Irish mythology, and is often a signal that one is about to work or walk between the worlds. Examples can be found in *The Voyage of Bran mac Ferbail*, his *Three Calls to Cormac*, and *Immacallam in dá Thuarad*. Highly shamanic in origin, it denotes the user's journey from one world to the next through the significance of sound and vibration.

In *The Voyage of Bran*, while out walking he hears the most beautiful music he has ever heard. He falls into a deep sleep; and, upon awaking finds a silver branch hanging from a tree in front of him. He returns home and, in front of the entire clan, a beautiful, ethereal, Otherworldly woman appears, telling him of the place where the branch originates, a land where it is always perfect summer. The next day Bran and a company of his trusted men make the voyage across the sea to find this land.

Many adventures befall Bran and his company as they travel to and spend time in the Otherworld. But time passes differently in the Otherworld, and what seemed like a year was more like hundreds. When Bran and his men finally return home they realise how much time has actually passed. Under a *geis* (magical restriction) they are not allowed to set foot upon the land, and when one of his men ignores this he turns to dust on the spot where his foot touches the shore. Bran tells the people of his voyage as they gather upon the shoreline, listening to this figure from legend. He and his men then sail away across the sea, and have been unheard from ever since.

This tale denotes the power and importance of the silver branch. It is not a tool to be used lightly, for travelling between the worlds can be a very risky business. As a symbol of the Otherworld, its sound and vibration call out across boundaries, allowing one to work and walk between the worlds. In today's modern usage, the silver branch is indeed used to travel between the worlds; however, it has other uses as well. It sets an intention, often used at the very beginning of ritual, calling our minds to the present moment, awakening our senses fully to this world before we enter into others. It can also be used to call to the three worlds, or as groundwork for journeying of any kind.

You probably won't find any silver branches that are already pre-made; you will have to make one yourself. This is not a difficult task, but one that should be taken with due care and reverence. Research and read all the myths and legends that you can find relating to the silver branch. Once you have some knowledge of its mythological origins, you will have a better grounding for your own personal use.

To make a silver branch, find a branch from a tree that appeals to you, one with which you may have a connection. Common trees used today are apple and oak, but you can use any tree that you feel will help with your ritual intention and work, that connects you to the Otherworld. If you are cutting live wood from the tree, make sure that you do so properly, using a sharp tool to make a clean cut and not damage the tree any further than needs must. Always, *always* make a connection with the tree first. Tell it of your intention, and really wait for an answer. If the tree is willing to let you take a living branch, then do so with full respect. If the answer is no, then accept it and look for another tree. You may always use fallen branches instead, which is my own personal preferred method. Ensure that these fallen branches haven't lain on the ground for too long, for they can become dry and brittle, or damp and rotten. Try to find some new branches that have fallen; going out after a storm is usually profitable. A good thing to note is how portable you want your silver branch to be: do you want to be able to pack it up in a bag and take it on a day's hike to a special spot, or put it in your luggage to travel long distances? Then you are going to want to find something relatively small and sturdy, that won't have little branches to snap off in your bag.

Once you have found your branch, you will need to find some bells to attach to it. The size of the bells will depend on the size of your branch, and your own personal taste. Do you want to make a lot of noise? Then larger bells are the ones for you, often obtainable around Yule for decorating your home, or even found on some antique horse harnesses. If a light tinkling will suffice (especially good for indoor use, when you don't want to disturb your neighbours, or your cats) then you can find tiny little bells from any craft shop that will work.

The amount of bells that you attach to your silver branch will vary, according to the branch that you have decided to work with. Numbers range from nine, thirteen, and so on, usually in denominations of three (a sacred number to the Celts, as in many other religions and cultures around the world). Find something pleasing to you, that works for you. You can attach your bells using leather thong (ethically sourced, of course) or coarse twine. Ensure that however you attach the bell, it is free to ring, not dulled by the leather or twine, or rattling against another bell or a part of the branch that will cause undue wear and tear.

And that's it for making a silver branch. It is actually very easy to make, and very simple. However, its use is extraordinary. When you use the branch for the first time, really be aware that you are making a call, a connection to the Otherworld. Unexpected things may happen. You are going to walk between the worlds, meeting with beings and encountering situations that may challenge you. Are you up to it?

There was a green branch hung with many a bell

When her own people ruled this tragic Eire;
And from its murmuring greenness, calm of Faery,
A Druid kindness, on all hearers fell.
W B Yeats

The Staff

All those wonderful, bearded old men in robes have one, don't they? Gandalf, Saruman, Radagast... Okay, they might not technically be Druids, but they look and act the part, don't they? All joking aside, the Druid's staff is an important tool in ritual, as well as being very practical when out hiking in the countryside.

In Welsh mythology, the god/magician Gwydion carries a staff made of ash. Ash is a tree often associated with the axis mundi, the world tree, spanning the worlds and being central to life. In Irish mythology we see the *bile*, a sacred tree or pole that was honoured in ritual for much the same reason. As another representation of a connecting thread between the worlds, the staff has both magical and functional uses.

Trees were and still are very important to the Druid tradition. In classical texts it is noted that Druids worshipped in sacred groves, called nemetons. Surrounded by this grove, the Druid was able to do her work, calling upon the powers of nature, the ancestors and the gods. Today we can see the symbolism of this reflected in our Druid's staff, a portable grove, if you will, that represents the sacred grove, other worlds and the connection to nature and the trees that are so important to our wellbeing.

The Druid's staff today may or may not be made of ash; it is purely your choice as to what kind of wood you would like to use. The type of wood may depend greatly on your home environment and what is readily available, if you choose to make your own staff. There are also gloriously carved staffs available from Pagan stores worldwide. What kind of wood you use or choose is important, and care should be taken when selecting. Research the myths and legends of the type of wood in Celtic lore, or that can be found in your native lands and from its mythology. Find out as well what the tree is like, from which you obtained the wood. What climate does it prefer? Is it a fruiting tree? How deep do its roots go? Does it live near the sea? Is it coniferous or deciduous? All these things will relate to the energy of the staff, its own energy and any that you wish to infuse it with.

If making your own staff, use the guidance above for the silver branch. Ensure that the wood is good and strong. Carve it if you like, smooth and polish it or leave the bark on. The size of your staff is again up to you; it can be as tall or as short as you wish, as thick and sturdy as you please. Bear in mind portability, if you wish to carry it around, and also whether you will be kicked off any public transport for carrying a staff that can be construed as a weapon. You may only use it for ritual purposes, but if you wish to travel and use your staff, these considerations will have to be kept in mind. In places like Glastonbury, England, it's not terribly unusual to see a robed Druid walking around with a large staff of wood. In Ipswich, it will only invite ridicule, curious looks and possibly the police. In all honesty, we have to admit that historically staffs not only have a stabilising function for walking, but they also double up as weapons should one be attacked. Pilgrims often carried staffs for this dual purpose, to help them on their journey and to protect them from harm.

As stated previously, my personal staff doubles as a walking stick, so I am able to carry it wherever I go without any funny looks. It was made for me by a lovely park ranger, who found a good, strong yet slender piece of hazel wood perfect for my height, just above the elbow. The bark, which is smooth, is left on, and the tip is rounded and sanded down. It is lightweight and easy to use in both ritual and walking. The hazel's connotation to the salmon of wisdom in Celtic lore inspires me in its ritual use.

In ritual, the staff can represent the sacred grove, a sanctuary and sacred space where transformation can occur. Simply by having your staff in the ritual you can call upon its connection to the grove. It can be used to cast the circle, if you wish, call to the deities, the three worlds, etc. The staff can be used to direct energy, or to contain it. You can put personal power into the staff and, depending upon the wood used, it can store up energy to be used in ritual. It is also a symbol of protection, as stated earlier, against things of this world and perhaps not of this world.

The Cup, Bowl or Cauldron

As a vessel that contains liquid, the cup, bowl or cauldron is often used in Druid ritual as a symbol of transformation. In its earliest form, the cauldron can be seen as linking us directly to the ancestors, where life congregated around the hearth fire, and the cauldron was a symbol of nourishment for the whole family. Within its depths, combined with the element of fire, food could be prepared and heating for the dwelling provided.

The cauldron also links us to the Welsh goddess Cerridwen, famed for brewing her special potion of awen within the cauldron of inspiration. As three drops accidentally fell upon Gwion Bach's finger, the magic transferred to him and he began his initiation into the mysteries. The Holy Grail is a later version of the cauldron, holding the power of life and death, rebirth and transformation. In actuality, any cup, bowl, chalice or cauldron is often used in ritual with various intentions, such as to hold offerings for the gods, ancestors and spirits of place. A cup or chalice might hold the ritual beverage for the feast, or it may hold water used to consecrate the space used for ritual.

The cup or cauldron is often linked to the feminine, associated with the transformative powers of the womb. However, the male god Dagda in Celtic mythology has a cauldron of his own, from which no man was left unsatisfied. The cauldron itself is honoured in ritual, but we must remember that it is the empty space inside that allows for transformation. We can liken this to seeking integration with the world around us, through a deep transformative experience where we can let our sense of self dissolve into the wider world of nature. In that emptiness, in the darkness of potential at the heart of the cauldron lays the deepest Druid mysteries.

Some have a ritual cup or cauldron used only for ritual purposes. Others see no separation between the sacred and the mundane, and find a link to their ancestors through practical as well as spiritual uses of a certain tool. You can find beautiful cups, cauldrons, chalices and bowls quite easily in charity shops and second-hand stores, as well as antique fairs and shops. They come in all shapes and sizes, made from all sorts of materials. Cups and chalices can be carved wooden creations, beautiful handmade clay designs, silver or pewter or even carved from stone. Cauldrons are most easily found in brass or bronze from antique and charity shops, and in iron from most Pagan supply stores. Find what material speaks to you the most.

Use the cauldron or cup in ritual for meditation, to brew something special, to place offerings or to consecrate the sacred space. You may have one vessel for each of these actions, but when out and about in the landscape it's probably not very practical to have all these to hand. We certainly don't want to be carrying pounds of extra weight in our ritual gear to a special site, and so a seashell or small lightweight wooden bowl can be used. You may also find a stone at your special site that has a hollow in it, perfect for leaving offerings, or using the rainwater collected within it for any sort of consecration.

The Drum

Many modern-day Druids use drums in ritual. Harking back to a more shamanistic expression of spirituality, drumming can be used to connect us with the Otherworld, much like the silver branch. It is often a tool for journeying, a meditation that allows the spirit to travel while the body remains in place. Drums can also be used to clear energy and consecrate a sacred space, or to raise energy within ritual.

Drums remind us of our heartbeat. When using a drum in ritual, we will often find our hearts begin to beat in time, responding to the sound and vibration that washes through our bodies. Within its rhythm we can dance, trance and meditate, communing with the gods, the spirits of place, the ancestors and more. It is a link back to the earth, and can be both freeing and grounding when used in ritual.

Drums come in all shapes and sizes, and from all sorts of materials. You can use the classic Irish bodhran, but this requires quite a bit of skill and co-ordination to use. The most often used drum in Druid ritual today is a circular hand-held drum with a soft beater for the other hand. However, drums of all shapes and sizes, and from all over the world, are used in Druid and Pagan ritual. If you find an affinity with a particular style, then go for it!

The ethics of sourcing your drum is a major consideration. This is a tool that will take your soul on journeys far and wide, and in so doing you will want something that has been produced ethically. Why entrust your soul to anything less? There are many handmade drums of natural materials such a wood and leather that can be found from ethical suppliers. With a little research, you can find a drum such as my own, crafted by a Druid friend using ethically sourced pony skin. There are many drums that use deer hide and cow hide as well, or even goat. Knowing that this leather was obtained from an animal that died of natural causes after living its life to the fullest will imbue the object with integrity. If you are not opposed to hunting for food, then you can use the skin/hide in order to fully honour the animal and its spirit. For those who are vegan, there are also many drums available that use a synthetic skin, and which produce just as high quality sound as animal skins. Again, the choice is yours to make. You can also make your own drum, and there are even make-your-own kits available.

Many speak of using the drum to ride across to other worlds.

This is why I chose pony skin for my drum, for my love of horses and for being able to use it to soul journey. When we choose an animal skin for our drum, we have to be fully aware of the energy and spirit of the animal that it comes from, for this spirit will help or hinder us in our work. If you choose a skin made of ethically-sourced deer hide, then be aware of what deer means to you, both in a spiritual as well as a practical sense. Read up on the type of deer; know its habits, inside out. Try to find something that is local to you, if possible. Go out and meet with the animal's brethren, if you can, in the physical as well as the spiritual.

I remember a Summer Solstice ritual that two friends and I performed impromptu out on the heath where I live. We walked across the sandy soil, through the gorse and heather and into a copse of beech trees. We began drumming, first softly and then more loudly, expressing our joy at the heart of summer's light, finding freedom and ecstasy within the drum/heartbeat. We danced and chanted, drummed, swirled and danced, me with my pony skin and they with their deer hide drums. All of a sudden a motion brought us a little out of our ecstatic trance, and there running up to us was a small herd of young fallow deer. Attracted to the noise, the energy, and the soulsong of their brethren, they graced our ritual with their presence. It was magical.

Drums can also be used for healing in ritual, and there is a popular method in many drum workshops that I've attended where one undergoes a soul cleansing or purification through the sound and vibration of the drum. The recipient stands in the middle of a group of drummers, and they begin to beat their drums from about a foot away all around the person, from head to toe, washing the entire body with sound. The beat is usually increased until the person in the middle is awash with the sound and vibration, allowing it to flow through the body and clear away any negativity or energy that is stuck. It is a truly powerful experience, one that I have undergone myself a few times, and it always leaves me refreshed and wide awake, renewed.

Sticks, Stones and other Fetishes

When out and about in the landscape, we will often come across little (or sometimes large) objects that seem to call to us, to ask us to pick them up, to study them closely, to take them home. It may be a bird feather on the forest floor, awash in a tiny pool of light, or a pebble on the beach that shines with a vibrant colour. It may be an unusual fallen branch, or a pile of shells from freshwater oysters left behind by an otter. These are all objects found in nature, that may have specific meaning for the individual, and which can be used as a power object.

A power object is not necessarily imbued with power in and of itself. It is in the connection to the Druid, the relationship that the Druid has with the object, that makes it powerful. It can connect us to a totem animal, for instance. At one of my favourite spots out on the heath where I live, there is a fox den near a copse of birch trees. When I go to visit every couple of months, I usually find something interesting just outside the den, as if waiting for me to pick it up. Having spotted the fox and offering a blessing to it once, as it spun away into the autumn heather, I feel that the fox is giving back to me in turn, even as I bring offerings and recite blessings to the place. I have found rabbit skulls and leg bones, crow skulls and interesting stones, right outside the den lying on the sand. Each time I collect an object, I bless the foxes and their home, praying for their safety from humans, wishing my beautiful cousins all the best as they live out their lives in the wilderness.

These objects that I have collected (or been gifted by the fox, as I like to see it) have no power in and of themselves, but rather have always appeared in my life when I needed to work with them. So, the crow skull appeared just as I took my Druid College students through the Realm of the Sky, and reminded me of the intelligence and wisdom needed to navigate the heavens, as well as laughter and perfect freedom. It is in the connection where the power is found, where the awen or inspiration in Druidry flows and we have sacred interaction. It is how we live and learn together in a functioning ecosystem, sharing the wisdom.

My altar is full of small fetishes, such as smooth pebbles from the beach near my home, old sharpened pieces of flint that fit perfectly in the palm of my hand (pre-historic cutting tools) found near ancient burial sites that connect me to the ancestors, feathers from the birds in my garden and out on the heath, pieces of sea glass and teacups found along the shoreline after a storm, quartz stones from dried streambeds, nine hazelnuts from a local wood and more. Each object has significance for me, reminding me of my connection to the land, the spirits of place and the ancestors. If an object no longer has significance, if the lessons have been learned and room must be made for new objects, then I return the items to the land with blessings and prayers of deepest gratitude.

Some fetishes are so small that we are able to carry them with us at all times. We can make a small pouch to wear around our necks to carry stones, twigs, small feathers and the like. We can keep small pouches of sacred objects in our handbags, or make amulets for places such as sacred sites. We can use these items for specific intentions, such as a protection amulet to hang in a car, or a collection of skulls around an outdoor temple area, similar to the way many Native American tribes return the spirit of the animals to a sacred place, working with them on a spiritual level and honouring the relationship. It is the intention you place when working with these objects that matters the most, not the thing itself, though it should be considered something sacred. Druidry is all about relationship.

Sickle and/or Knife

A popular image in Druidry is of white-robed priests climbing a sacred oak tree to cut down mistletoe with a sickle (a curved, hand-held blade), catching it in a white cloth before it touches the ground. This singular account comes from Pliny's *Natural History*, and has instilled itself in the imagination of people everywhere. Pliny states:

> *The druids – that is what they call their magicians – hold nothing more sacred than the mistletoe and a tree on which it is growing, provided it is a hard-timbered oak. Mistletoe is rare and when found it is gathered with great ceremony, and particularly on the sixth day of the moon. Hailing the moon in a native word that means 'healing all things,' they prepare a ritual sacrifice and banquet beneath a tree and bring up two white bulls, whose horns are bound for the first time on this occasion. A priest arrayed in white vestments climbs the tree and, with a golden sickle, cuts down the mistletoe, which is caught in a white cloak. Then finally they kill the victims, praying to a god to render his gift propitious to those on whom he has bestowed it. They believe that mistletoe given in drink will impart fertility to any animal that is barren and that it is an antidote to all poisons.*
> Pliny, *Natural History*, XVI, 95

Though Pliny is the only person to have recorded such a practice, therefore inviting speculation among historians as to the accuracy or validity of his accounts, Miranda J. Green in her work *Exploring the World of the Druids* advocates the legitimacy of his accounts based on the importance that the oak and mistletoe has in Celtic mythology and artwork. Mistletoe was also known as 'all heal', and today has been proven to have many beneficial medical properties. It was more than likely that the Druids had a special ceremony for the harvesting of such an important herb, and their love of trees and worship in sacred groves all provides links back to Pliny's account. Whether or not you actually believe Pliny or not, the sickle is a common tool found in Druidry today.

Pliny's account of using a golden sickle is odd, for gold is not a strong enough metal from which to make a cutting blade. What the sickle was most likely made from was bronze, polished to shine like gold, but able to cut through the herb. Gold just sounds better. You can find many sickles of all sizes with bronze or even steel blades from antique shops. I picked mine up for only £8. It has a lovely handle that I think is made from either beech or oak wood, but it is hard to tell as its colour has changed over many long years of use and oil from human hands. Its blade is not sharp, and I do not require it to be, for it is used as a ceremonial item only. For me, it is a connection to the Celtic Druids of the past, as well as the people of this land who have used it to harvest many things throughout the seasons of the year. I cast the circle with my sickle. (See Chapter Four for more details on circle casting.)

There are many images from 19th century artists, evoking a romantic image of the Druids, both male and female, with their sickle, robes and mistletoe. If this is an image that appeals to you, and which you'd like to explore further, then I encourage you to find your own sickle, and listen to the stories that it has to tell you.

If you are going to be out and about in the landscape for any length of time, it is usually quite handy to have a knife with you. If you are harvesting herbs, or wood for a ritual tool, or using it to trim branches into a form of tinder to light a fire, then the knife is quite a vital part of working in any landscape. Knives in the Druid tradition are not usually associated as strongly with magical workings as they are in the Wiccan tradition. Knives can certainly be used in this way, to cast a circle or for other ceremonial purposes, but essentially knives are functional tools used for cutting, trimming, carving and the like. The choice is yours.

If you are going to use a knife, either for practical or ritual purposes, then you must ensure that you are carrying one that conforms legally to the laws of your area. I don't require a large hunting knife when out and about in the woods where I live, for I am never really gone long enough or out far enough in the wilderness to warrant it. If I am going on a long excursion in the wilds, then I will certainly take my Swedish knife that has a larger blade, but which is still legal in most countries for blade length. At all other times, I carry a tiny penknife, a mini Swiss Army knife that has a good, sharp, 1 inch blade, as well as scissors, file and toothpick. It has come in handy on very many occasions, and I can carry it in my pocket or in my handbag. It's even been through airport security, because I forgot to take it out of my handbag once! I was so glad when I realised afterwards, when I had got home, that it hadn't been confiscated.

Be careful and practical with all knives. If they are for working use, keep them sharp but not too sharp, for then they will become brittle. Find out the legalities of your area, for even if you are walking around with a completely dull-edged knife, if the blade length isn't legal, it can be taken away from you.

Robes

I've mentioned the accounts of white-robed Druids a couple of times already, and this is the popular image still of Druids today. However, Druids wear robes of any colour they wish, if they even wear robes at all.

There is something about putting on a special item of clothing to mark a sacred occasion. In secular culture we have special 'dress' clothes for weddings and funerals, for example. These are not everyday items, but something for a special occasion, something out of the normal routine. Ritual robes can be viewed in much the same manner. Slipping into a ritual robe before the rite can focus our minds from that point onwards that we are performing a ritual. We feel different. The ritual has begun, so to speak.

Many modern Druids use robes in ritual, usually made from natural materials for their connection to the earth. As well, natural cloth won't usually go up in flames instantly, or melt onto the skin should it come too close to a fire. Natural fabrics are more breathable as well, though there are some manmade materials such as Gore-Tex that allow for breathability, but also keep out the rain. I've often wondered if Druids here in the UK should have ritual raincoats, as it rains so often on these wonderful isles!

Ritual robes are usually made to look like something from the past, to connect us with our ancestors or to provoke a romantic image that is pleasing to the eye. Some Druids have ceremonial plaids to honour their clan heritage, and wear that over their robes or everyday clothes in ritual. Other Druids look into history and archaeology for ancient clothing to provide them with inspiration on what they can make that will be similar.

Some modern Druids do not have ritual robes at all. Many prefer to wear modern clothing, and it is rather more practical if you are going out hiking across the wilderness to a sacred site rather than wearing long, flowing robes that you have to hold up around your knees, getting sleeves caught in bushes and so on. I only wear ritual robes when performing ceremonies for others, such as when I am called upon to perform a handfasting for a couple, or a child's naming ceremony, or a funeral. I always ask if they would prefer me to wear my special robes or not, and have several different colours to try to match the mood and/or colour scheme. So, I have a set of blue cotton robes for summer, a set of grey robes in linen, and a set of black woollen robes for winter. My woollen robes have been a blessing in zero degree Celsius ceremonies, where the frost covered everything in beautiful white, glinting in the slant of late winter sunlight.

Otherwise, I wear the clothes that I have worn that day. If I am going out onto the heath, I always make sure that I am wearing good boots, as I live in adder country. I have seen many of these beautiful snakes, and they are usually lovely and shy, but just in case I step on one by accident, I'd like to have some protection. If it looks like rain, I will wear a waterproof coat with hood. In the snow, I have my snow boots and pants, ski jacket or heavy winter coat, gloves and mittens. I like to think that my ancestors would appreciate me wearing practical clothing when going to visit special sites, rather than freeze my buns off in other ritual gear. I'm sure if the Celts had jeans, they would wear them too. (Interesting note: the Celts developed trousers!)

If you are going to wear ritual robes, choose a colour carefully. Keeping those white robes white while out and about in a muddy field could be quite time-consuming (not to mention the environmental impact of any bleach you may use). Natural, earthy colours are always a good idea. Some colours relate to a particular grade of Druid, such as for the Order of Bards, Ovates and Druids where they use blue robes and/or a tabard for Bards, green for Ovate and white for the Druid grade. Other traditions don't have grades at all, and so anything that appeals to you will work. The Romans have recorded accounts of black-robed female Druids on the isle of Anglesey, casting their magic and performing their rituals just before the Romans invaded. You can research the symbolism and meaning of different colours, but do be aware that there are many different systems and interpretations of colours. You will have to find one that feels right for you.

Altars

Altars are great focal points for an area where you perform ceremonies, meditate, or simply commune with nature, the ancestors or the spirits of place. Then again, as with all tools in the Druid tradition, they are not absolutely necessary, as all of nature can be our altar, our focus. However, I usually find it helpful to have a smaller focus from which to work, as I can't physically hang out with the entirety of the UK landscape at the same time.

You can create an altar anywhere you like, provided of course you have permission from either the landowners or spirits of place. I have several altars, one indoors in my spare room, another one outside in my garden, and one at an ancient burial site a couple miles' walk from my home. I use my indoor altar when I need a more comfortable and secure, quiet space to work, or when it's absolutely tipping it down outside and I'd rather not meditate in the pouring rain. (Although I have done this as well, and it's lovely, but perhaps not in the middle of winter.) My indoor altar is also an homage to the sanctuary of the hearth and home, of the space where I live, these four walls that shield me from the elements and give me a safe place to rest my head at night. My outdoor altar relates directly to the spirits and ancestors of place, all the things that live and pass through my garden, including the bees and blackbirds, the deer and pigeons, neighbouring cats and badgers from down the way. It is also a focus for those who have lived on this land before, human ancestors who, according to the deeds of the property – which date back to the reign of George III – lived in 'hovels' here in the former apple orchards. I listen for their stories in the twilight, and look at the apple trees that were replanted here in the garden, feeling the song of this place and all those who have gone before. My other altar at the burial site is one that is used by a few unknown people (our paths have never crossed), and it has a fire pit and a few logs to sit on right next to an ancient tumuli. Fire itself is the altar, the focal point for ritual at this site.

An altar is a personal thing. It can hold all your Druid tools and objects, as well as photographs, artwork and more. It can represent a microcosm of the place where you live, or be dedicated to a particular god or goddess. It can be an altar for the ancestors, or even working with a specific element or realm, such as the Druidic triad of land, sea and sky. You may even have several altars in and around your home, each with their own purpose.

An altar can be made of any material. My indoor altar is an old blanket box that is never used, laid out with candles and my ritual tools, artwork and fetishes. Outside in my garden, the altar is a flat stone laid atop another stone, with an incense holder bearing a triskelle (triple spiral) motif, a small statue of the Morrigan, some stones from the beach and a lantern with a small tea light candle. Every week I bring an offering to this altar, and at the eight festivals of the year, or when something important has happened in my life. The offering is usually bread with butter and honey, and maybe some wine or whiskey tipped onto the earth. The plate is always empty the next day. As stated above, my third altar is a fire pit, working with the ancient energy of fire that was so important not only to our Celtic ancestors, but to humanity as a whole.

When choosing a site for an altar, ensure that you have permission from the landowners, if you do not own the land, as well as the spirits of place. Placing an altar on land that is not your own without permission from either is just asking for trouble. You want to work in harmony with the land, and not be seen to be claiming a space for your own, or even raising suspicion from other people in the area as to strange ritual practices and goings on. Always work with respect and common sense.

Fire/Candles

Fire has always fascinated humanity. It is a beneficent as well as a destructive force. It is transformative.

The Druids are documented as having several different fire ceremonies according to the classical writers. The most famous is the burning of a wicker man, an effigy given over to the flames as a sacrificial offering. Three ancient sources (Caesar, Strabo and Posidonius) document this ritual, in which it is said humans and cattle were packed into a wicker cage and burned alive as an offering to the gods. Whether or not this is true or simply Roman propaganda, we will never know, but the custom of burning straw effigies continued until the 19th century in many parts of

Europe. These were, of course without the human or animal sacrifice and were more of a folk tradition. Indeed, it is quite a sight to see, as I recall at one Druid Camp (held during the cross-quarter festival of Lughnasadh) a Green Man was built with branches, twigs, flowers and other greenery in the centre of a labyrinth, its paths lit by a hundred little tea lights in lanterns. An archer from outside the labyrinth took a flaming arrow and shot it into the effigy, setting it alight. It was spectacular.

Offerings, prayers and sacrifices are often made with the transformative power of fire. Needless to say, modern Druids no longer sacrifice anything that is alive in their ceremonies, leaving that to our Iron Age forebears in an era where that made more sense. Nowadays, we offer petitions and prayers into the flames, watching as the fire takes them and transforms them, the smoke rising up to the heavens. The Green Man effigy at the Druid Camp ceremony mentioned above was an honouring of the green and growing things, and an acknowledgement of the turning of the cycle from the Summer Solstice, as the wheat and barley had ripened in the fields under the fire of the sun, the power of the green and growing had reached its height and was now descending into the dark half of the year.

The cross-quarter days in the Druid tradition are often also known as the fire festivals. Imbolc, Beltane, Lughnasadh and Samhain all have fire as the central focus, albeit in differing degrees and forms. Perhaps the most popular are Beltane and Samhain, still strongly celebrated as fire festivals today, as evidenced by the society called the *Beltane Fire Festival*, active in Edinburgh, Scotland, during the times of both Beltane and Samhain. Hundreds of people gather in a theatrical display of ceremony, where a sacred fire is lit, providing a connection back to our ancestors of the times when similar fires were lit at these sacred points in the year.

As stated previously, your altar can consist of nothing but a central fire, the flames acting as a focus for transformative ritual.

If you are unable to have a fire, then candles can be substituted, providing you with access to a flame in a more appropriate setting. A single candle burning in the darkness is wonderful and meditative, allowing for deep change to occur. Fire is a powerful tool for change.

When we haven't got the space for a fire, whether outdoors or indoors in a lovely fireplace, we can use candles instead. There are many different types of candles that can be used to honour fire or have it as the central focus in your ritual, from beeswax tapered candles to seven-day candles in glass jars. The safest candles to use indoors are in storm lanterns or the large jars, as these are very hard to tip over, either by your own hand, a cat jumping on the altar or a child running past. If they do tip over, they will simply go out. Ensure that you take all safety precautions with candles indoors, such as not having them near curtains or anything that can go up in flames, or not too near sensitive fire detectors as the smoke can sometimes set them off and ruin the ritual atmosphere. If using candles outdoors, again storm lanterns are the best option, to stop them from going out in the slightest breeze. There are also battery-operated tea lights that resemble flickering candles, but as batteries are terrible for the environment, I wouldn't suggest using them in Druid ritual. As well, try to buy candles made from beeswax or soy instead of the usual petroleum-based ones. These will be a little more expensive, but you can use them for special ritual occasions, and so they will last a long time.

Incense

The smell and smoke from burning herbs, resins and gums not only takes us back to our ancestors, who have been doing so for millennia, but can also take us immediately into a ritual frame of mind, signifying that ritual has begun.

There are three different types of incense that can be used in modern Druid ritual today. These are cone, stick and loose incense. Cone and stick incense are just that; herbs and resins that have been rolled into a stick or cone shape, that can be lit and held in special containers to catch any falling ash. Loose incense consists of resin, gum and different herbs that can be burned singularly or together on a small charcoal disc or briquette held inside a fire-proof container.

Many people prefer loose incense in ritual, as it is more in keeping with what our ancestors used. However, for indoor ritual the smoke that it produces can simply be too much, and can set off fire alarms. Also, the container that holds the charcoal disc that the incense is burned upon can become very, very hot, and is a fire hazard in and of itself. Animals or children can burn themselves or knock it over, causing havoc.

Loose incense is wonderful for outdoor ritual, as it isn't contained within a small space and won't smoke out an area. You can even just throw a small handful of homemade incense onto the coals of a fire, and watch as the smoke rises, scenting the air with its magic. Again, all hazards when using candles, incense or fire should be considered, wherever you are.

The charcoal for burning incense should be from a reputable dealer, and there are companies that sell such from ethically sourced materials. Excelsior Charcoal Tablets, for example, are made from cuttings taken from fruit trees, and therefore no trees are cut down for the making of their little discs/briquettes. You will also have to consider that burning charcoal releases carbon monoxide in larger quantities than stick or cone incense, and so ventilation is always something to think about where charcoal is being used.

I prefer to use stick or cone incense. Stick incense is extremely portable, and can pretty much be used anywhere, indoors or out. There are wonderful inexpensive wooden holders for indoor use, that also can store sticks in a little compartment below the actual burning area, keeping everything you need all in one place. They have covers and lids so to protect anything from touching the smouldering end, and are available in many different and pleasing carved patterns. I believe these are the safest for indoor use, with cones second and then charcoal third. Stick incense can also be used outdoors, by pushing one end into the ground. It is very transportable, and easy to use. Look for handmade stick incense from various different suppliers, as these will contain real gums, herbs and resins as opposed to the factory produced ones that usually are just chemically perfumed sawdust.

Incense can be used to consecrate a ritual area, used alongside the cup that holds water. In this regard, the realms of land, sky and fire are honoured with the incense, and the realm of the sea within the water of the cup/bowl.

Chapter Four

Druid Ritual Elements

An nì a thig leis a'ghaoith, falbhaidh e leis an uisge. (What comes with the wind will go with the water.)
Irish Gaelic proverb

What follows is an exploration, piece by piece, of the different elements of modern Druid ritual, in the order that they are usually performed. Not every element is done by every single Druid across the globe, and indeed as Druidry is a religion without liturgy, ritual is essentially what you want it to be. There are no hard and fast rules, no 'what you should or shouldn't do'. However, there are elements that many in modern Druidry follow today to give a sense of cohesion, especially when doing public ritual together. They provide a structure or framework that the Druid can use in a shared language that most will understand if they have studied the Druid tradition at any length. The elements of modern Druid ritual are as follows, usually done in the order shown:

1. Call for peace
2. Casting the circle/creating sacred space (preparing the nemeton)
3. Honouring the spirits of place
4. Honouring the ancestors
5. Honouring the three worlds
6. Honouring the deities
7. Ritual intention and action
8. Prayers, magic
9. Offerings and Eisteddfod
10. Feast
11. Closing

The Call for Peace

Inspired by the writings of Iolo Morganwg (Welsh poet, antiquarian, collector and inspired literary forger of the 18th and 19th centuries) the call for peace begins many modern-day Druid rituals. Regardless of the validity of Iolo Morganwg's writings, the call for peace is a very good concept. It is more of a prayer for peace at the beginning of every rite, and tries to establish whether there is peace, both within and without.

Wicca has the saying 'in perfect love and perfect trust', and the Druidic equivalent would the call for peace. I've personally always been more comfortable with the call for peace rather than the Wiccan version used in some mixed Pagan rituals I attend, as I find it hard to establish perfect trust in ritual with people that I perhaps do not know or have only just met. However, I can always assert that there is peace.

The call for peace is a petition, that there may be peace from all four quarters of the globe, north, south, east and west. It also asks that there be peace in our own hearts and minds, and compassion towards all life. It establishes that there is peace in the ritual between participants, whether they are other humans gathered together for ritual, or the lone Druid enacting ritual with the spirits of place, the ancestors and the gods as witness. Druid ritual is never something that is completely performed alone, for there is always nature, all around us, all the time. We live in a shared reality with myriad other beings, and so we acknowledge them and pray for peace.

The call or prayer for peace is also a much-needed reminder of how we need calm in our culture, our society and our world. There are wars being fought, people being attacked, politicians lying, animals being abused. We pray that peace can be found so that we can begin to heal, both ourselves and the planet, from the devastation that humanity has incurred.

It is also a reminder that peace begins first and foremost with ourselves. When that peace is found, it will naturally radiate outwards into the wider world. From a calm, stilled centre we are able to act with intention, instead of reacting to the world around us. Ritual is an opportunity to stop, to pause and to honour the time and place of our being in the world, and the world itself.

The call for peace can be as simple as facing each direction and saying the following:

May there be peace in the north,
May there be peace in the east,
May there be peace in the south,
May there be peace in the west.
May there be peace in our hearts and minds, and toward all fellow beings.

Sometimes the call for peace is done in a different order, to symbolise the equal-armed cross that features in much of pre-Christian culture. So, it would start in the north, then south, then west, then east, and finally turn into the centre.

Not every Druid uses the call for peace, but it can be a wonderful way to start a ritual, and in many group rituals you will find that they begin with this petition. Incorporate it into your own ritual if you so wish, to help you find balance and harmony.

Casting the Circle/Creating Sacred Space

When using an area for Druid ritual, whether indoors or out, it is always a good thing to ask permission from the spirits of place first and foremost. You wouldn't want just anyone walking into your living room and doing ritual there, would you? It's only polite, at the very least, to ask the spirits of place for their permission. This may not always be necessary at a site that you work with regularly, as you will have felt your presence to be accepted. But if you are moving to a new site, or a new location within your home, it's always wise to check beforehand whether it will work for everyone, seen and unseen.

It can be as simple as the following:

Spirits of place, I ask for your permission to use this site for my Druid ritual. It is my intention to honour the times and tides of life, to dance in your beauty and energy, to give back for my bounty.

Wait, really wait and *listen* for an answer. The answer may not come in the form of a voice, but rather in a feeling of acceptance, a peaceful feeling that all is right. If you do not get an answer, then perhaps this is not the place, or the right time to work here. Or, ask again, gently, really focusing on your words and listening for an answer. Sometimes we're just too excited or nervous to formulate our intention clearly, or to listen/feel for a reply.

Use your intuition to find a good space for ritual. If outdoors, you will need to consider privacy, as well as whether or not you are working on someone else's land. If so, you will need the landowner's permission. Some urban Druids work in city parks, other Druids work by the seashore, some find ancient stone circles while others prefer the deep heart of the forest. Find out what appeals to you, and what you can easily access in your area. If you have to drive 50 miles to reach a suitable area, then perhaps you need to find something a little closer to home. Druidry is all about locality, working with the place where you live, being a part of an ecosystem and learning from it. It can be your backyard if necessary, or a balcony of an apartment building under the moon. Druids usually work out of doors, really connecting with the natural world no matter what the weather, dependent upon their ability. Do what you are physically capable of doing to get outside, even if it's just to sit by an open window. That being said, you can always perform Druid ritual indoors, if necessary.

Now we move on to creating sacred space. It must be said, that in Druidry there is no unsacred place. Everything within nature is sacred. However, by creating a temple to honour the sanctity within nature, we are able to perhaps hold a focus a bit better, working with a microcosm of the universe in our ritual space. So, 'creating sacred space' is a term often used, but perhaps 'working with sacred space' might be nearer the mark. Most in Druidry use the term creating sacred space, and so we use it here.

The classical writers commented that Druids worked in a grove of trees, called a nemeton. Here they performed their rituals and made their offerings and sacrifices. The nemeton means sanctuary, a space where we can feel safe, where we can stretch and work our Druid ritual for deep transformation. We delineate the bounds of an area within which we will work, and in doing so create a temple of sanctuary wherever we are. We ourselves are at the heart of the nemeton, at the heart of the circle, and aspects of ourselves and our souls radiate outwards from this central core. Where we find the edges we find the areas that require the most work, being furthest away from the core. These are also the edges where souls meet, where soul touches soul and relationship occurs.

Indeed, there is a goddess of sanctuary and sacred space, known throughout Celtic lands in Europe and Britain: Nemetona. She is an elusive goddess, with only hints as to her being, and a few inscriptions on altars. She can also be found in place names and tribe names. For more details on the goddess Nemetona, see my work *Dancing with Nemetona: A Druid's Exploration of Sanctuary and Sacred Space*.

To create this sanctuary in which to work Druid ritual, we use the energy of the place combined with our own personal energy. We 'cast a circle' by walking the boundary edge of our ritual space, and combine our own energies with that of the spirits of place. We might begin by standing within the centre of our space, and saying the following:

> *Spirits of place, of the beech tree who stands proud, the blackbird and the crow, the green grass and the earth beneath my feet, the clouds high overhead, the brilliant sunlight through the dappled leaves, I ask you to help me create my circle, layering it with your intention, that the circle may be strong.*

We then walk the boundary of our ritual space, and we may use our staff or an outstretched hand to push out our own personal energy, layering it with the energy of the spirits of place. As we walk, we may say something along the lines of:

> *I create this sacred space as a temple to honour the spirits of place, the ancestors, the gods. May this nemeton be safe and secure; may it be blessed with rich potential.*

The power of the edge of the sacred space depends on what you put into it. If you want to create a loose circle where energy can flow freely in and out, then you can do so with your own intention. If you wish to create a place that is separate from the outside world, you will need to 'cut the threads' that connect you to the outside world when you delineate the edge of your sacred space. Instead of creating a line of energy, energy that is combined with the spirits of place, you can 'cut' or separate the outside edge of the circle from the rest of the world, using visualisation as well as personal power. You can use your staff, or a knife if you so wish, to cut the threads. This is usually reserved for deep, transformational ritual, for magic or for protective rituals. A looser, more open circle is preferred for celebration, such as for the eight seasonal festivals or to honour the moon's cycles.

Once you have walked the circle's edge, you can then wrap it around, stretching it into a sphere if you wish, so that you are held in a 'bubble' so to speak. You can also tie a knot when you come back to the starting point of the creation of the circle's edge, and just leave a circumference as your temple boundary. The choice is a personal one.

The ritual space is then usually consecrated. This is an act that demonstrates the sanctity of a place. When using an outdoor space, we are not so much 'purifying' the area, but acknowledging its sacredness, seeing it as the microcosm of the earth, of the three realms of land, sea and sky, of the four elements of many Pagan traditions of earth, air, fire and water. It is like saying a blessing on the area, hallowing (to honour as holy) it for use.

We can consecrate an area in many different ways. The most traditional in Druid ritual is to carry incense and water around the circle. The incense represents the elements of earth, air and fire popular in a lot of modern Paganism, or the realms of land and sky with sacred fire in the Druid tradition. We then have water carried around separately, representing, of course, water or the realm of the sea in the Druid tradition. You can carry the incense around first, wafting it with your hand or a feather and say:

I bless this area through the powers of earth, air and fire (or the land, sky and fire).

You can also sain an area with a smouldering bundle of dried herbs, such as mugwort, instead of using incense.

Next, you then carry around the water, scattering drops, and say:

I bless this area through the powers of water (or the sea).

That being said, if you are out in the wilds of nature and don't have incense, herbs, water or other items to consecrate an area, there are other ways to do so. You could drum, sing, or chant for example. Some Druids don't feel any need to consecrate a ritual space, especially outdoors as they see it as a practice of purification that is unnecessary in the wild. Consecration largely depends on how you view the action, whether it is ritual purification, a blessing or an acknowledgement of the sacred (or all three).

Honouring the Spirits of Place

The temple has been created, and now the spirits of place are honoured. Here we say a few words about the beauty and wonder where we are performing our ritual, and allow our deep love and reverence for the earth to blend with our words, truly honouring all that surrounds us. Druidry is a religion of locality, and so each and every day the Druid honours the environment where she or he lives, working together with the spirits of place to find a way of living that is in balance and harmony with the ecosystem. The Druid seeks to find deep relationship with locality, so that everything that is done in that place works for the benefit of the whole. It is an acknowledgement of the shared reality where we all live, and the Druid might say something along the lines of:

I honour the spirits of place, of beech and birch, of the frogs in the pond, of the songs of humanity that flow through this place. I honour the wind that blows through the trees and around the houses, the sky overhead, the stars hidden by the light of day. I honour all that share this place and this time with me.

Honouring the Three Worlds

Now we come to the place where we honour the three worlds of land, sea and sky. The three worlds (and triplicates in general) are an important part of Celtic religion, and as such are still honoured today in Druid ritual. Sometimes honouring the three worlds takes the place of honouring the four quarters found in much of modern Paganism, other times it is done either before or after. In this work I will provide both, and allow you to include whatever seems best for your own rituals.

For the Celts, the land held the domain of plants and animals, humanity and geographic features. Trees and forests, rocks and stone circles captured the imagination of the Celts and were held in high regard. The sea was often the abode of the ancestors, an underwater realm honoured in many ancient Druid rituals as attested by the artefacts found in watery locations like lakes, bogs and marshes. There is even a tree henge in Norfolk, built right next to the sea, and which has now been claimed by water, visible only at certain low tides. The sky belonged to the gods of nature such as Taranis, the Celtic god of thunder. It is also the place of fire, where gods of the sun such as Aine were honoured. As stated previously, smoke from fire carried many an offering to the sky realm, allowing petitions and prayers to travel between the worlds.

What links the three worlds together is the *bile*, the sacred or world tree that has its roots in the deep springs and waters of the Underworld, its trunk in the Middleworld and its branches in the Upperworld.

As a religion that is a native tradition of the British Isles, Druidry is heavily influenced by its locality. As an island, surrounded by the sea, with a vast range of geography ranging from wetlands to mountains, dry heathland to deep ancient forest, the presence of the three realms is all around us, at all times. We begin by honouring the land, the firmness and stability on which our lives are played out. We then move to the surrounding seas, which hold the land and nurture it. Then we honour the skies overhead, the sunlight and rain that we depend on for our very existence. We can see calling to the three worlds or honouring the three realms as not only an external appreciation, but reminding ourselves and reawakening our consciousness of them within our own selves. We might say something along the lines of:

I honour the three worlds of land, the sea and sky. May our foundation be strong as the mountain. May our love be as boundless as the sea. May our inspiration reach as high as the sky.

Honouring the Four Quarters

Here we call to the four quarters of the globe, a practice that is found in much of modern Paganism. Within our ritual space, we acknowledge each of the directions and all the associations that we have made with those directions, letting it further layer our circle in a microcosm of our world.

There are many agreed associations with each direction; however, as Druidry is a religion or spirituality of locality, these may not be appropriate for you in your ritual. If you prefer to follow an agreed standpoint, then that's perfectly fine, but if you feel you need to change an association so that it better reflects your environment, then that is all well and good. For instance, I live on the east coast of Suffolk, in the east of England. If I face east in my ritual circle in my backyard, I face the North Sea. In much of modern Paganism and Druidry, the west is usually associated with all the aspects of water. However, to the west of me lies a big chunk of this landmass known as England and Wales, with a further hunk of Ireland in the way before we come to the Atlantic. So, east for me means water.

I'll go through each of the four quarters and their usual connotations in modern Druidry here, and then you can use or adapt them as you see fit. In ritual, we usually say the words as we face the direction and allow our associations to fill our ritual space, blending our psychic soulmap onto physical reality for ritual.

We begin in the north (though some Druids begin in the east). The north is the place of cold, of darkness. It is the stillness found in a leafless tree. It is a place of frost and ice, of cold winds and death. It is also the place of rest, where the seed lies dormant in the rich dark earth. Indeed, north is associated with the element of earth, honouring stability, a strong foundation, the hearth and home as well as family. Some of the animals that are associated with the north are bears, owls, badgers, moles, bats and wolves. The season is winter, the time is midnight and the festival is the Winter Solstice. It is the place of dreaming. If we look to ancient associations with Celtic Ireland, north is associated with battle. Many great warriors such as the famous Cu Chulainn were trained in Ulster, which is the northern province in the structure of Celtic Ireland. To invoke the north in ritual, you might say something like the following:

I call upon the Spirit of the North, the Great Bear (constellation and sacred animal), *the cold winds of winter, the strength of the warrior, the darkness of midnight, of the womb, of potential, to be with me in my sacred rite!*

We then move to the east, a place of light and creativity, of new beginnings. It is the place of the rising sun, of awakening. The east is associated with the element of air, honouring freshness, communication and inspiration, the breath of life. Some of the animals relating to the east are the hawk, eagle, butterfly and bee. The season is spring, the time is dawn and the festival is the Spring Equinox. It is the place of planning, of thinking. In Celtic Ireland the east is the province of Leinster, with associations of prosperity, hospitality, contests and feats of arms. To invoke the east in ritual, you might say:

I call upon the Spirit of the East, the Noble Eagle, the dawn's light, of new beginnings and prosperity, of inspiration, to be with me in my sacred rite!

Then we move to the south, a place of the greatest light, where the heat of the sun brings all green and growing things to their full height and majesty. It is the place of passion, of action and of strength. Animals relating to the south are the stag, the dragon, the serpent and the boar. The season is summer, the time is noon and the festival is the Summer Solstice. It is the place of action, of doing. In Celtic Ireland we find Munster in the south, the place of music and teaching, wisdom and poetry, fierceness and fertility. To invoke the south in ritual, you might like to say something similar to:

I call upon the Spirit of the South, the King Stag, the brightness of the midday sun, the warrior's fierceness, the heart of passion, to be with me in my sacred rite!

Finally, we come to the west, the place of the setting sun's light upon the water. It is a place of rest, of the ancestors and wisdom from deep springs. It holds the realms of emotion and transformation. Animals relating to the west are the salmon, the kingfisher, the otter, heron and swan. The season is autumn, the time is evening and the festival is the Autumn Equinox. It is the place of rest and contemplation, of reaping what you have sown. In Celtic Ireland we find Connacht to the west, the place of knowledge and counsel, history and beauty, abundance and wealth. To invoke the west in ritual, you can try something similar:

I call upon the Spirit of the West, the Salmon of Wisdom, the light of the setting sun, the wisdom of the ancestors, the tides of love, abundance and knowledge, to be with me in my sacred rite!

Sometimes a fifth direction is called in Druid ritual, being the centre. It is the place where all directions meet and overlap, where we find the deep honesty of our very core being. The knowledge of the centre is the knowledge of sovereignty.

Some Druids who only celebrate at the cross-quarter days of

Imbolc, Beltane, Lughnasadh and Samhain honour the times when the associations linked to the four quarters meet each other. So, for example, if we associate north with the element of earth, and east with the element of air, then Imbolc is the point of the year where earth meets air. At Beltane, air meets fire, Lughnasadh fire meets water, and Samhain water meets earth.

Honouring the Ancestors

In Druid ritual we honour the ancestors, those who have gone before and our ancestors yet to come, our bloodlines and our teachers. This is another triplicate, as we honour the ancestors of place, of blood and of tradition.

The ancestors of place are those who have lived on the land before us, both human and non-human. They are in the soil, in the earth beneath our feet. Their stories are those we can hear on the wind, singing back to us through the mists of time. It is important to look closely at the area where you live, and try to discover its history and archaeology. Learn about the ecosystem as much as you can, find out what has changed, what has remained the same over many long centuries. What animals have lived there before, and still live there now? Their blood and their bones are what make up the soil in our back gardens and parklands, forests and heaths. Their life and their death are wrapped up with our own, and we must remember that we too will become an ancestor of place.

The ancestors of blood are those humans from whom we have descended, whose stories flow through our veins, who give us our DNA. We could, of course, go all the way back to the first homo sapiens and beyond in honouring the ancestors of blood, but most prefer to narrow down the focus to the past few hundred years. For example, in 10 generations or less we can have more than a thousand ancestors, from all over the world. What we can do is begin our focus on our immediate family, our parents and siblings, grandparents and so on. We can talk to them, and if they are still living, learn their stories, which are also our stories. To go back further, we can even use DNA testing, such as at ancestry.co.uk or ancestry.com, where we can trace our family histories online, connect with people and also even take an ethnic DNA test to see where our ancestors have come from the past 500 to 1,000 years. The results may surprise you!

The ancestors of tradition are our spiritual ancestors, our teachers and our guides on the Druid path. They may be living or dead, real people or even mythological heroes. What is important is that we have learned something from them, and continue to learn by honouring them for what they have taught us. They may even be from a different tradition. For example, one of my ancestors of tradition is Zen monk Thich Nhat Hanh, whose writings and work have inspired me to live mindfully in the present moment, and do all that I can towards creating a world of harmony and peace. I also honour my teachers of the Druid tradition, those whose words and deeds inspire me on my own personal journey. We might find historical figures that fire our imaginations, and that speak to us on a soul deep level, such as Boudicca or Martin Luther King Jr. What matters most is that they have taught us not only about ourselves, but also about the world we live in.

Words used in ritual to honour the ancestors can be as brief or descriptive as you would like. What I use for most ceremonies is the following:

I honour the ancestors of place, whose songs flow through this land. I honour the ancestors of blood, whose stories flow through my veins. I honour the ancestors of tradition, whose wisdom flows through the teachings.

As with all aspects of ritual, we not only say the words, but we feel them as well, their associations with our lives and the connection that they have to the wider world.

Honouring the Deities

Deity in Druid ritual is a very personal thing. As a religion or spirituality that has many gods, acceptance of this is a wonderful aspect of group ritual. Being in a circle where there are devotees of Danu, flamekeepers of Brigid, worshippers of Cernunnos and more is inspiring in its open declaration of tolerance. I have also been in circles with Christian Druids and Buddhist monks, as well as other religions from all over the world. Acceptance that there is no single path to deity is a large part of the defining element of Druidry.

When in group ritual, if there are many different followers of many different deities, then the words used in honouring them in ritual become more inclusive and less specific. We might say something as simple as:

We honour the deities, all the gods and all the goddesses whose followers have gathered here in this ritual.

You could also use a more generic invocation to the deities, delineating aspects of them that are common threads throughout much of modern Paganism. If so, you could use something like the following:

I call upon my Lady of the Stars and Moon
To the Bringer of Dreams and Twilight
I call upon my Lady of the Loom
The Weaver of Fates in the night
I call upon the Lady of the Lake
The Singer of the Evensong
I call upon the Maiden, Mother, Queen and Crone
The Goddess alive and strong

I call upon the Lord of the Sun
The Rider in the Sky

I call upon the Lord of the Winds
To the Eagle as he flies
I call upon the King Stag
To the Son, Lover, Hunter and Sacrifice
I call upon the Lord of the Wildwood
The God laughing, free and wise

In solo ritual, you can be as specific as you like when speaking words to honour the deities. Indeed, your deities may not even have a name, as they may simply be the gathering of forces in your local area: the forest, the heath, the valley. Such unnamed deities could very well have been a large part of ancient Celtic religion, as local tribes honoured local deities, the names of which may have been lost or changed over the millennia.

If you wanted to be very specific, you could say something like this (or sing it, as this is a personal invocation to deity that I sing in solo ritual or to greet the day):

Brighid my Lady, your voice I hear
Within my soulsong I draw you near
Flame of my heart I feel your fire
Sacred water beneath earth and sky
Springwater rise

Brighid my Lady, I honour you
Goddess of this land and awen too
Inspire my soul with your sacred art
Feel my heart beating as I feel your heart
It's where we start

Brighid my Lady, so strong and true
Can you feel my love flow straight unto you
Green-mantled goddess guide my way
White Serpent Lady to you I pray

Each and every day

You may also use ritual actions, gestures and movements when calling to the deities to honour them in ritual. Song and dance can also be used, as we are trying to enchant the deities as much as they have enchanted our very own souls, so that we can be inspired by them and express our love for them in ritual.

Many Druid rituals are performed simply to experience the deities in the ritual setting, calling to them and allowing them to inspire us. Druid deity is all about nature, and opening yourself to the powers of nature that are flowing all around you. This is often where the aspect of prayer comes in, which we will discuss later.

Ritual Action

As stated above, sometimes the point of ritual is simply to open ourselves up to the powers of nature that inspire us to live our lives in accordance with our love for them. The ritual action then might simply be quiet meditation, opening your heart to them. It may be a time of peace and quiet, set apart from the everyday world of noise and machines, chores and obligations.

Then again, we might have a very specific purpose to the ritual, such as celebration of one of the eight festivals of the year. Taking time out to acknowledge the changing seasons, the tides and times of life on a regular basis helps us to attune to the natural rhythms and cycles of life. If this is the purpose of the ritual, then we say the appropriate words and perform ritual actions to honour the time of year. While it is beyond the scope of this work to go into all eight festivals and their meaning, I can provide a brief example here. For more information on the eight festivals, please see my other Pagan Portals book, *The Awen Alone: Walking the Path of the Solitary Druid*.

For a ritual to honour the Autumn Equinox, we might say the following while scattering fallen leaves around the circle, or walking slowly with the sickle held aloft, or holding the first apple of the season:

> *I honour the growing tides of darkness, where now the nights are longer than the days and the air turns cool. The harvest is still coming in, and we come face to face to reap what we have sown. At this magical time I celebrate the changing of the seasons, the turning of the wheel. I prepare for the coming winter, as my ancestors did, working hard so that the harvest will be bountiful. All around me nature is preparing for winter, the birds migrating overhead, the hedgehogs and squirrels fattening in the hedges and under the trees. I steady my soul as I look to the western shore where I hear the voices and songs of my ancestors.*

We might be performing a ritual for healing, and so using any number of methods to direct the energy of the rite towards this end. We might simply soak up the energies of the place, the deities or the three worlds and in doing so heal a part of ourselves. For the use of magic in ritual, such as in healing, we will discuss this further below.

We might use chanting, drumming or dancing as the ritual action to connect with the time and place we are honouring.

The intention of the ritual may simply be to give thanks for all that we have. We may have received wonderful blessings or news, or just be deeply inspired by the beauty of the sunset.

Whatever the intention of the ritual, when performing the ritual action, do so with full mindfulness. Be in the present moment, awake and aware to all that is happening around you. By being fully present, any words that you speak, any gesture or movement you make will flow more easily, be more graceful and filled with meaning than those done with a wandering mind. This is an opportunity to really connect with the land, the ancestors, the deities and your own self, and so it deserves our full attention.

Prayers and Magic

What usually follows, or takes the place of ritual action, is prayer. Many rituals are conducted simply to reconnect with the gods, the spirits of place, the ancestors and so on. There are many different types of prayer, from thanksgiving as stated above, to petitions for help or healing, to simply speaking of your love and devotion to the deities and the land. We may simply be questing for the awen (searching for inspiration in our lives) whether generally or specifically related to a problem.

A prayer that I often use in ritual is that of opening myself to the power of my Lady Brighid.

I lay myself upon the anvil of Brighid.
May my soul be tempered with experience,
May my heart be strengthened by compassion,
May my thoughts be shaped by love.
May I walk forth anew with the blessings of Brighid:
The forger and the flame.

If we are offering a prayer of thanksgiving, we might say something like this:

I give my thanks for the bountiful harvest. The wheat has come in safely from the fields, despite the threatening rains. Thank you to my lady of the sun and to my lord of the growing grain.

We might petition the gods or ancestors for help in a specific problem:

Ancestors of tradition: awaken within me compassion and inspiration for learning how to deal with difficult people in my life, others that are contrary and dishonourable in their dealings with me.

We might pray for healing, for ourselves, for the environment or for the world.

May we find peace and healing in our hearts and minds, and may we all work together towards a life that is honourable and integrated, respectful of each other. May our wounds be healed, our differences set aside and our resolve to work together strengthened with each passing day.

Prayer might become a magical act. When we combine our own energies with those of the earth, we can create a magical working that weaves prayer and magic together in a combined wave of energy directed towards its goal. We might research healing herbs that our ancestors used, such as vervain, and toss a handful into the fire while praying to the gods for healing. By holding the herbs in our hand, pushing our energy into them and visualising the desired effect, then combining that with the following words of prayer, it becomes a magical act contained within Druid ritual.

Herb of healing, sacred vervain
Herb of the ancestors, take this pain
Herb of earth, herb of fire
Help me win my desire.

As Druidry is a religion or spirituality of nature, we acknowledge both our own power and that of all nature around us. It is in the combination of personal and natural energies that magic is performed and created, and using the tool of visualisation to direct the energy, it manifests towards your desired goal.

There are accounts of the ancient Druids performing magical rituals, such as at Anglesey where it was recorded that wild female Druids ran to and fro along the shoreline, chanting and shouting curses at the Roman warriors who stood on opposite, awaiting the order to attack. This might very well have been a magical ritual to stop the invaders, which sadly did not succeed.

Take the time to investigate ancient records of Druid magic, as well as exploring modern ways of combining personal and natural energies. Many Druids don't perform magic at all in their rituals; however, if it appeals to you then it certainly isn't something that goes against tradition in Druid ritual throughout the millennia.

Again, as it is beyond the scope of this introductory work into Druid ritual to delve deeper into prayer and magic, please see the bibliography and suggested reading list for more on these subjects.

Offerings, Eisteddfod and Sacrifice

After prayer and/or magic or the ritual act we make offerings to the gods, the land, the spirits of place and the ancestors. Druidry is a tradition that is based on relationship, a give and take that places us firmly in an environment, in the present moment, working in balance. We know that if we take too much, we will suffer. We also know that if we give too much, we will suffer also. The oak tree provides a home for myriad beings, food in its acorns and leaves, oxygen, shade, wood and more. It doesn't give too much, for it will compromise its existence in doing so. But still it gives, freely, willingly, as it is a part of an ecosystem working towards the survival of the whole. If only humanity could be as wise as the oak tree.

Offerings are usually made in the form of food and drink. Organic, homemade food and drink would be well suited to the Druid tradition, but this isn't always an option. We have to consider the impact that any food left out will have on the environment. Chocolate is not a good offering, as it has an ill-effect on many animals. Most sugary things save for honey will not do wildlife much good. If you are tipping drink onto the ground, consider what you are putting on the ground. Will hard alcohol be detrimental to the plant life in area? Dependent upon your own tradition, there are food and drink that have long associations with particular deities, the Otherworld and its inhabitants. Research and meditate on what would be a suitable offering in your area.

Offerings may also be in the form of an expression of creativity. This is called the Eisteddfod in the Welsh tradition. It usually takes the form of sharing poetry and song, music and dance. There is even a National Eisteddfod every year in Wales. It is the expression of creativity, in the flow of awen, the giving back of the inspiration we have received, that is most important in this regard. The awen must always flow. Sing a song you have written particularly for this ritual. Play your tin whistle to the sea as it rolls along the shingle shore. Recite a poem that inspired you throughout this season. Remember, it is in the doing, not the thinking that Druidry is enacted.

Sometimes offerings are replaced with sacrifice, and this is a loaded term for many people. We are not here to appease the gods, but to develop a deep relationship with them, with the land and with the ancestors. We may be reminded of Roman accounts of Druids performing human sacrifice, or divining the future from the entrails of birds. Regardless of whether this is simply Roman propaganda or not, it is simply not necessary in today's world. Today we use the term sacrifice to denote a ritual action where an offering is simply not enough. Sometimes, to get deeper into that relationship, we make some sort of sacrifice. This may be in a form similar to an offering, but the difference lies in the significance of the object. The Celts sacrificed beautiful, unused swords, shields, jewellery, chariots and more, later to be found by today's archaeologist in lakes and bogs throughout Celtic lands. To spend hours creating these objects, to dedicate their time and effort must have been an immense undertaking, and then to give them over to the gods was indeed a huge sacrifice. We can do likewise, in offering things that are important to us, whether in the form of an object, or our time and energy. The importance is on the energy spent, the effort involved, the physical, mental and spiritual impact, which is usually much greater than the usual ritual offering.

Feast

The feast can be seen as a grounding of the energy towards the closing of a ceremony. It is a time for reflection and for allowing the purpose of the ritual, its actions and words to flow through our bodies, instilling the wisdom and the teachings of nature that continually flow around us. It allows us the time to settle, to find our balance once again, and begin the return to life outside of the ritual.

By eating and drinking we bring our psychic awareness back into our bodies. It may just be a bite of food and a sip of drink, but in doing so we are also sharing what we have been given.

Before we eat or offer any food and drink back to the land, the ancestors, spirits of place or the gods, we can recite a short blessing and then leave a portion out for them, such as:

From the earth and sun, from the wind and rain, I offer this back to the land again.

If we don't have any food or drink, as for instance when we find ourselves in an impromptu ritual out in the wilds somewhere, then we can do another form of grounding to bring us back into sync from the energy of ritual. We may place our hands upon the earth, allowing the earth's energy to stabilise and ground us in the present moment. We might clap our hands three times, signalling the return to the everyday. We might take three long, deep breaths to return our awareness back into our bodies. What matters most is that we create a signifier that the ritual has been done, and that we are now going to begin closing down the rite.

Closing

The closing of a ritual is done in the reverse order to that which set up the ritual. It is a time of offering thanks and blessings, and taking the opportunity to deconstruct the ritual space, one element at a time, so that we can return fully into the present, allowing the work that we have done to spill out into the wider world.

We begin by thanking the deities, then the ancestors, the four quarters, the three worlds and the spirits of place. We might say words like:

I give my thanks to my Lady Brighid, green-mantled lady of this land, for Her many blessings and for being with me always. I give my thanks to the ancestors, to ancestors of blood, of place and of tradition.

Turning to each of the four quarters in turn, perhaps in the reverse order to which they were called, we can say:

I give my thanks to the Spirit of the West, the Salmon of Wisdom. I give my thanks to the Spirit of the South, the Great Stag. I give my thanks to the Spirit of the East, the Hawk of Dawn. I give my thanks to the Spirit of the North, the Great Bear.

We might reach down to touch the earth, saying:

I give my thanks to the land, for its nourishment and stability.

We might then stand with arms extended sideways, and say:

I give my thanks to the sea, for its protection and enchantment.

We might then raise our arms to the sky, and say:

I give my thanks to the sky, for the inspiration and the awen.

We then give thanks to the spirits of place.

I give my thanks to the spirits of place, who have watched, witnessed and been a part of this ritual. Know that you are honoured.

We then take down the circle that we have created, whether it is a circumference or sphere of energy, in a similar manner to that which it was made; if casting with the staff, silver branch or knife, we would use that same object to draw the energy back in. If we cut ourselves off from the external world, unravelling the threads that connected us instead of pushing our energy out in a protective boundary, then we must reweave those threads.

Finally we ask the spirits of place (if they have helped create our circle as previously in this section) to release the energy, with gratitude.

I give my thanks to the spirits of place, to the grand beech tree that stands guardian, the blackbirds singing in the twilight, the frogs chirping in the pond. I ask that you release what you have offered in my circle casting, to allow the energy to flow free.

Now we formally acknowledge the end of the ritual, and the changes that have taken place. You might say something like:

This ritual ends in peace, as it began. Now that the sacred circle is released, may what we have witnessed and created here flow into the wider world, to be shared amongst all who dwell in it. May what we have seen and heard here be an inspiration to all. May we all be blessed by the awen, the inspiration that is the spark of life, the courage to live it and the flame of love to guide us in its flow.

Chapter Five

Altered States

Cha dèanar sagart gun fhoghlam, 's cha dèan foghlam sagart. (A priest should be learned, but learning won't make a priest.) Irish Gaelic proverb

Ritual is often enacted in order to provide us with an altered state, where our consciousness shifts from the everyday into a world that is more expansive, where the enchantment is real. We can become so single-minded in our perspective, and when going into altered states of consciousness we expand that perspective, giving us many other different points of view from which we can learn, transform and work. We will now look at a few different kinds of altered states, which by no means are the only paths to this goal. Attaining these altered states may indeed be the ritual action, to whatever purpose, held within the safety of the ritual circle.

Meditation

Meditation is often used in religions all over the world as a way to calm the mind and retune the body. Within Druidry, meditation is used for this same reason, as well as for journeying and problem-solving. We will look at these three aspects of meditation, and for more information please see the list of recommended reading at the end of this book.

Meditation as a tool for calming the mind and retuning or relaxing the body has been used for thousands of years. It is often done before prayer, so that our prayers will be clearer in their intention. By achieving a calm mental state we are often better able to asses a situation, our lives and the world in general. By working from a place of intention, rather than reaction, our words, thoughts, behaviour and deeds will be more in tune with the tenets of Druidry and the natural world.

There are a quite a few ways to achieve this calm and relaxed mental state. One of the most popular is the Tree Meditation. Find a comfortable place to sit, either indoors or out, on a chair or on the ground. What is important is that you are comfortable, and that your circulation won't be compromised in any way. After years of sitting in the 'easy pose' of Buddhist meditation, I find this the most comfortable, with my right leg folded inwards towards my cushion, my left leg folded in after it. I sit on two cushions on the floor so as to raise my hips, as when your hips and knees are in line you will have created a very stable platform to sit in for any length of time. My back muscles have been strengthened through hours of sitting without a backrest, and it may take some time if you aren't used to meditating to develop those muscles. Persevere unless it is painful. However, if you ever feel pain then stop the pose and find a way to be more comfortable. My hands usually rest on my thighs, sometimes palms down, sometimes palms up, sometimes in certain mudras (hand positions found in Eastern traditions). Do what feels comfortable for you.

Take a few deep breaths, really focusing on the air flowing in and out of your lungs. Try to breathe through your nose if this is comfortable. Once you have begun to settle down, on your next exhalation visualise a long taproot extending from the base of your spine, down into the ground. With each exhalation, send that root further down, down into the soil, reaching the dark, cool, moist, rich earth. When you have reached that point, on each exhalation send out side roots in all directions, anchoring your taproot to the spot. Do this for a few breaths, and then finally send out tiny little hair-like roots from these side roots upon each exhalation, little hairs that search for nutrients in the soil.

Spend a few moments simply breathing down with each

exhalation into your roots. Then, after a while, on an inhalation, breathe in from the roots, breathing the loamy scent of the earth, the nourishment from the soil. Exhale back down into your roots. Breathe in from your roots, and out through your roots, for as long as you wish.

This meditation is excellent for grounding work of all kinds. You may like to end the meditation here, if you require a deep grounding. However, you can extend this meditation a little further.

Now, instead of continuing to breathe down into your roots with each exhalation, you can shift to exhaling through the top of your head, creating a canopy of branches, a crown of leaves above you just as you created your root system. Breathe in from your roots, and exhale into your canopy, spreading it as wide as is comfortable. Continue with this breathing for several moments. See what it feels like to draw in nourishment from the deep earth, and release it into the sky.

Finally, when you are ready, begin to draw first your canopy and then your roots system back into your body with each inhalation. End with the final drawing in of the taproot back into your spine. Once all your roots have been taken in, simply sit and focus once again on breathing in and out through your lungs, returning your mind to the here and now. Listen to the sounds around you, the smells. Wiggle your fingers and your toes, roll your shoulders and when ready, slowly open your eyes, returning to the present moment.

You may find that your spine is tingling from the energy of breathing to and from it, allowing the body's energy to flow freely. This is a good thing, as energy needs to move freely!

Journeying is another form of meditation often used in Druidry, where the meditator goes on an inner journey. We might be seeking a deeper connection to our ancestors, or to the spirits of place, the gods, the sidhe and other denizens of this world and the Otherworld. There are many tales in Celtic mythology of a hero journeying, usually over water, to gain wisdom and insight into their lives (in Celtic Irish myth known as *immrama*). Today, we might be seeking allies from this world and the Otherworld to work with in the future. In the following journeying meditation, we will go to find a spirit ally, perhaps an ancestor of tradition, who may be able to guide us in our future work.

Sit in your meditative posture, and take three long, deep breaths to cleanse your mind and body. Allow your thoughts to quieten, and once you are ready begin the following visualisation.

You stand at the edge of a lake, the still water reflecting the sky above. Hanging on a small tree next to you, you see a silver branch, much like the one you own. You reach out and take the branch in your hands, shaking it three times. You then return the branch, and it slowly fades from view. Turning your gaze to the lake, you see a mist begin to form. The mist comes closer to where you are standing on the shoreline. Out of the mist, a small, flat-bottomed boat appears, paddled by two cloaked and hooded figures. Silently the boat approaches the shore, and stops with a soft bump upon the edge of the lake.

One of the figures turns and stands up, reaching out a hand to help you into the boat. You take the hand and step into the vessel, moving to the front where a small bench awaits you. The figures behind you silently push off from shore and paddle the boat into the awaiting mist.

You feel the mist all around you and its cool, soft, damp touch upon your skin. It surrounds you, and you are adrift in this strange sea, where the light has no source, the directions have no meaning. All you can feel is the boat steadily moving forward, through the mist.

Slowly, the mist begins to recede in front of you. The light changes, and you can see a form looming ahead. As the mists fully part, you see before you a beautiful island. Green hillsides dotted with sheep and cattle roam up the banks of a tall tor, a hill that rises out of the landscape. Around the base of the tor you see trees, marching down to the water's edge. A little way off to the right you see a small clearing, where a tiny village has been settled in the arms of the forest, the tor standing guard. The boat begins to move towards the village, and soon you see a small landing dock jutting out into the lake. As you approach the dock, a figure moves from the shoreline and onto the platform. Cloaked and hooded like those guiding your boat, the form moves to the end of the wooden dock and awaits you.

Your boat pulls up, and is neatly tied to the dock by your navigators. The figure on the dock extends a hand to you, and you are pulled up onto the platform above the water. You look into the figure's face, and slowly the figure lifts its hands to the cowl of the robe and pulls down the hood. The figure smiles, a face that is neither old nor young, with eyes full of the ages of wisdom. 'Welcome,' she or he says.

From there, you can make many journeys back to that land, to learn from this person. You can visit the village, climb the tor, wander the forests and dive into the lake. With this person as your guide, you can learn the wisdom that they have to offer. When you feel it is time to return back to your body and your time, simply thank your guide, place an offering perhaps at a sacred shrine or in a place of beauty and take the boat back to the shore from where you began the journey. As you step out of the boat, you see the silver branch again in the boughs, and you shake it three times to signal the end of your journey. Then slowly begin to focus once again on breathing in and out through your lungs, returning your mind to the here and now. Listen to the sounds around you, the smells. Wiggle your fingers and your toes, rolls your shoulders and when ready, slowly open your eyes, returning to the present moment.

Meditation can also be used for problem-solving. Indeed, you can use the above journeying meditation to talk about a problem or difficulty with your guide in spirit. You can talk to the gods, the ancestors or the spirits of place, if you so wish. Alternatively, you can simply sit and focus on calming the mind first, and then attend to the problem in the proper frame of mind.

Take three deep breaths to calm the mind and bring your focus into your body. Allow your muscles to relax, and allow your thoughts to settle. If a thought comes into your head, allow it to arise, and then see it drift away. Keep allowing any arising thoughts to drift away until you have reached a place of quiet calm, where the mind is dark and rested.

Now, bring the problem or difficulty that you are having to the forefront of your mind. Still in your calm and relaxed state, look at the issue from all angles, from all perspectives. See it as an outsider would, who has no attachment to it at all, no preconceptions or judgements. Ask yourself some questions to gain deeper insight into the matter, such as, 'What has brought this about?' 'What is within my control, and what is not?' 'What, if anything, can I do right now to solve this problem?' If there is nothing you can do about it, focus on letting go of the need to control, and simply find an acceptance of the situation. If there is something that you can do, calmly and rationally think about the outcomes of your decisive action. Focus on what is best for all, what will create harmony. Find a solution that allows the ecosystem to flourish. If there is no solution to be found, then allow that to be as well. Sometimes there just aren't any answers. Time and tide will tell the outcome of any situation. Then slowly begin to focus once again on breathing in and out through your lungs, returning your mind to the here and now. Listen to the sounds around you, the smells. Wiggle your fingers and your toes, roll your shoulders and when ready, slowly open your eyes, returning to the present moment.

I hope that these examples of meditation will help you as you learn to work with altered states in ritual. As stated previously, there are many different types of meditation that you can use, so please do research the subject more fully and try out different techniques to see which suit you best.

Drumming

We've covered many aspects of the drum in the Druid's tools section, but here we will touch more upon the use of the drum for achieving an altered state of consciousness in ritual. The drum is often used for journeying, a term that describes a form of meditation or altered state where we can travel in spirit to other realms. The drum is often that which can carry us across and between the worlds, riding the drumbeat to new perspectives.

When drumming, you will find that you usually have a 'signature' beat that resonates with you that you keep coming back to. This is often a sequence of beats that is in tune with your own heartbeat, and as everyone's heartbeat is at a slightly different rate, it will be unique to you. It may be slow, it may be quick, but it is a rhythm that you find yourself returning to, time and again in ritual. Allow yourself to ride that sound, as it is an extension of your soul. Don't think that you aren't being creative enough in your drumming, but instead really explore that sound. You can get fancy later.

It's usually good to meditate before drumming, to ground, calm and centre your thoughts. As you are preparing to take a journey, it's a good opportunity to remind yourself of where you are now, before you go off on spiritual adventures.

When drumming, you don't necessarily need to create a lot of noise. Soft drumming can induce trance-like states that are just as effective as a loud pounding. What matters most is the intention behind the drumming, not necessarily the skill or the sound level. As with all musical instruments, however, practice does help to create a pleasing sound, and if you find that you have trouble keeping any sort of rhythm, you might like to attend some drumming workshops that will be able to help you steady your hand and your beat. If you find that you have absolutely no propensity for drumming at all, you can always listen to a drumming CD instead, and allow that to take you on a journey. Alternatively, if you have a friend who is a capable drummer, you could ask them to drum for you in your ritual as you journey between the worlds. Agree a length of time, and the type of beat with any changes in rhythm that you would like to use beforehand, as well as the signal to return.

Allow the drum beat to wash over you, to become your whole world. Let it sink into your body and fill your consciousness. Once you can feel the drumbeat within your body and soul, you can then direct the sound to take you where you would like to go. You can ride the sound to the Otherworld, to meet with beings that may be able to guide you on your path. You can allow the sound to take you deep on a journey to the Underworld, or deep within your own mind, to confront shadow aspects of yourself. The possibilities are endless.

Chant and Song

Enchantment is a large part of Druid ritual. If we look closely at the word, we can break it down into *en chant*: French for 'in song'. We are a species that, like many others, loves the power of song, of music. If we can be 'in song', if we can be enchanted, then we can not only find deep, transformative ritual and experiences, but also move between the worlds.

If you are blessed with voice, you can sing. If you don't like the sound of your singing voice, you can work on it with some lessons and tips (classes or even free online workshops) or you can always chant. Either way, using our vocal chords can help us to achieve an altered state in ritual.

Think of one of your favourite songs, and how it makes you feel to sing it. Does singing it change your mood, your emotions?

Does listening to your favourite singer produce an effect on you, physically, mentally and spiritually? What other songs have a similar effect on you? For me, the song of the blackbird, the Druid *dubh*, is a song from these British Isles that connects me instantly to Otherworld, reminding me that it is always here, always lying close to ours, and we are able to pass through and communicate with it should we so wish. At the liminal time of twilight, when it is neither light nor dark, day nor night, the blackbird's song opens the veils between the worlds.

Just as we have a signature drum beat that corresponds with our hearts, so too do we have a signature song, a melody, a tune that we keep coming back to, that holds great meaning for us. It may be something that we have created, or something that we have heard that strikes a literal chord within our souls. We love this song, we keep singing it, and in singing it finding the beauty and enchantment. We can ride the waves of this song to other realms, to other places of being, to widen our perspective, to take us out of our bodies and out of ourselves, experiencing life on an even grander scale. In song: enchantment.

Then again, we may prefer chant to song, in the anglicised meaning of the word. This is usually a repetition of words or a phrase, or a combination of phrases using less notes and melody than a song would contain. It is simpler, sometimes even monotone. It can be as elaborate as a Gregorian chant, or as simple as whispered words, over and over again to the rising moon.

Chanting and singing allow us to turn off our brains for a while, to stop the thinking and simply be in the moment. When we turn off our thinking, we can step beyond our boundaries and judgements, our criticising and our doubting. We can simply experience things on a profound and yet very simple level.

I would encourage you to write your own songs and chants, to use in your ritual practice. Try singing or chanting part or all of the ritual elements, from the call for peace to the closing rites. Use notes or a melody that you love, from your favourite songs or chants, or something that you have made up yourself. You might find your whole ritual changes, simply with the addition of song and chant as part of the ritual elements. You can also use it in the ritual action, to travel and journey into altered states of consciousness. However you use song and chant in ritual, I guarantee it will be something both beautiful and wonderful.

Sensory Deprivation

We can find various references to sensory deprivation as being part of the Celtic spiritual practice. These take on differing forms, the most common being exposure to utter darkness, or in a sweat-lodge called *teach-an-alais*.

Spending time in darkness, perhaps in a quiet, dark room or deep within a cave, or even blindfolded, has an effect on our psyche. We rely on our physical sight so much for input that when we take that sense away, we open ourselves to other senses, but also find a space to get back in touch with our own sense of self. In Celtic literature of the 5th to 8th centuries, there are accounts of poets/diviners/Druids who would spend hours in the darkness, resembling the darkness of the womb, and then be brought out into the light where they gave their prophecies. In the Irish tradition this is known as *imbas forosna*.

When we are released from distraction, we are better able to access those deeper areas of our soul. In darkness is where all life begins. When we are then brought out into the light, the potential that the darkness has held turns into manifestation. Performing *imbas forosna* is a perfect example of this.

If you have a particular issue, or a question that you would like answered, or perhaps simply want to become better attuned to your sense of self, your place in the web of life, then spending time in utter darkness can help you achieve clarity. This is, of course, best performed at night, and during the time of the dark moon, as it is the greatest time of darkness.

Find a place where you can eliminate all sources of light, if possible. A room indoors is probably the safest place, where you can draw the curtains and blinds. A cave out in the wilds is ideal, but of course all safety precautions must be taken first. You don't want to be sharing this space with anyone or anything else! If you can't achieve utter darkness either indoors or out, then take a cloak or a blindfold with you. You can wrap yourself in the cloak, or lay it over you to shield out all light, or simply place the blindfold over your eyes.

You can do this in a ritual circle, which would be the best place for such workings. You have the information you need already, so why not go ahead and use it for this ritual intention? It could offer up a wealth of information, solutions or inspiration in your life. Feel free to say prayers beforehand, drum or meditate. Then, simply lie down and spend time in the darkness, allowing your thoughts to slow down over time. If you fall asleep, do not worry, for this too is a powerful form of work. When you wake, tell yourself the story of what you have just dreamed so that you will remember it. Then, after a few hours or at dawn, whether you have stayed awake or just woken up, throw off the cloak, tear off the blindfold, open the curtains and roll up the blind, immersing yourself in the light of day. See what impressions, thoughts, feelings and emotions strike you as you move from darkness to light. After you have undergone this experience, journal it right away so that you won't forget any of it.

The sweat lodge, or *teach-an-alais*, is another form of sensory deprivation, where we shut ourselves off from the world and use the power of water and fire to bring us to another state of being. Beehive-shaped stone buildings have been found along rivers in Celtic lands and are perfect for holding in heat and providing a sacred place to journey, to heal and to cleanse, shut off from the outside world.

Through the power of water and fire, both held sacred in all Celtic lands, we can move from the everyday into the extraordinary. We can strip away the layers of our self to find our root souls, hidden beneath years of negative thoughts and experiences.

Research ways of building your own sweat lodge, through the natural materials that you have around you. Alternatively, you can buy saunas already made, or simply turn your bathroom into a similar experience. You can run a very hot bath (not scalding, of course, but quite hot) and sit in it for an hour. You should work up a sweat. It probably won't be as dramatic as a stone and peat-built sweat lodge, but the intention is the same at any rate.

It goes without saying that if you are pregnant, suffer from breathing or heart difficulties, then using a sweat lodge is not recommended. It is probably best to ask your doctor first if you are thinking of doing a sweat lodge, if you've never done one before. Drink plenty of water before and after your sweat lodge experience, but ensure that it's not too cold and don't over drink, i.e. downing two pints of water in one go. Take it easy.

Get the area to a hot enough temperature that you are sweating within a few minutes of sitting there. Ensure that it is not too hot that you will become faint, or not hot enough that you are comfortable. The point of this exercise is to experience some discomfort, but in a good way that releases or strips away the dross to reveal the truth within. Turn off the lights and either just have the fire in the centre of the sweat lodge or some candles in the room around you. If you have stones that you can pour water over to make steam, then go ahead. If you are in the bathtub, the steam from that should suffice. You can always top up with more hot water as necessary.

Close your eyes and breathe. Feel the heat on your skin. Feel the sweat coming out of your pores. Concentrate on the reason why you are here. Allow the sweat to strip off what is unnecessary. Come back to your true self. If you have a question, ask it as you allow yourself to sink into the powers of water and fire, of darkness and light. Do what you have come to do, and then when ready, stand up slowly and make your way out of doors, if possible. If you are near a body of water, dip your body in the water briefly, or roll in some snow. If indoors, rinse your body with cool water. Note what you think and feel as you do this. It is similar to *imbas forosna*, where instead of moving from darkness to light, you are also moving from heat to cold. Record your thoughts, feelings and experiences in your journal as soon as you can.

Sacred Landscapes and Sitting Out

A Druid is a part of a landscape, no matter where that Druid finds herself. Whether he lives in the rural countryside or in the midst of urban sprawl, he knows that he is part of an ecosystem. Every day he attunes with that ecosystem, for it is a part of him just as much as he is a part of it. To know that ecosystem is to know himself.

Taking ritual out of doors and connecting to the landscape is a very important part of the Druid tradition. We may take our crane bag with our special items, or we may carry nothing with us but our prayers. What matters most is that we do get out there, out into the landscape as much as we can.

If you are lucky enough to be mobile, try to find a place within your own landscape where you can perform your Druid rituals. Consideration must be taken in public spaces, with regards to land ownership and a host of others. Let your intuition guide you to find that special spot, that hums with energy and that calls to you, that you find yourself returning to time and again when out for a walk. It may be a quiet corner of a city park, or near an ancient burial mound in the countryside. It might be a grove of trees on the edge of a meadow, or by the seashore. It should be a space where you feel safe and secure, comfortable enough to practise your spirituality without interruption.

Working in a special place over a length of time creates an energy that can build up, allowing ritual to flow even more smoothly, to empower rites and to feed back to the land that provides us with so much nourishment. It is about finding and sustaining a deep relationship with the land. This special place can be thought of as your altar to the gods, the ancestors and spirits of place. It is a point of focus where you can work with and give back to the land.

Our Neolithic and Celtic ancestors knew the importance of such places, marked as they were often by stone circles and henges, created for whatever purpose was needed. We needn't always return to ancient sites, and indeed we can create new ritual sites where we can honour all that we hold dear. New ritual sites are opening up across the country, and in many people's private backyards. I have a very small stone circle set up in my back garden, where I meditate and pray. I also travel to an ancient tumuli, which is about a four-mile round trip by foot. There, I connect with the Sidhe, the fairy folk, the ancestors and the Otherworld on a deeper level.

Once you have found a suitable outdoor ritual area, spend some time there just being. Sit and allow the landscape to speak to you. Talk to it of your hopes and dreams, what you wish for the land. In the Norse tradition there is a term, *utiseta*, which means 'to sit outside'. If convenience allows, sit out in your area overnight, or for a day and a night. Watch the sun rise and set, feel the patterns that flow through the land. Create your ritual circle (after asking permission of the spirits of place first) and see how your energy combines with the energy of place. Get to know the flora and fauna of the area first hand. Which way do the birds travel in the morning? What walks past at dusk? Which scents linger in the air?

Take your rituals outdoors, under the heat of the noonday sun and beneath the light of the moon. Know your landscape in all seasons. It will be well worth it, for so will you come to know yourself.

Conclusion

I hope that this work has helped to enrich your ritual work in the Druid tradition. It is based on decades of personal experience and research, and has been offered to you in the spirit of awen, of inspiration. May the inspiration continue to flow, may your ritual work nourish you and the land itself. Awen blessings on your journey.

Glossary

Awen: Welsh word, meaning flowing inspiration or divine inspiration

Cauldron: A vessel that stands on three or four points, or which is hung over a fire, which can be used for cooking. Also prominent in mythology all across Europe.

Crane: Large, long-legged and long-necked birds that hunt for small fish

Druid: Traditionally a priest of the ancient Iron Age Celts, now denoting a follower of the Druid tradition in the modern day

Eisteddfod: A part of modern Druid ritual, where poetry, song or other forms of creativity are shared. Also a national event in Wales.

Fetish: An item usually of natural origin, such as a stone or feather, used by earth-based traditions as ritual tools or adornments

Goibhne: Irish blacksmith god

Imbas Forosna: Meditation in utter darkness, with revelation occurring upon stepping out into the light

Manannan: Irish god of the sea

Nemeton: A sacred place, a grove of trees where ancient Druids worshipped

Nemetona: Goddess of the sacred grove

Ritual: A prescribed set of words and actions within a particular context used to bring about a desired outcome, often repeated over time

Sain: To bless or consecrate an area with either water or smoke

Shamanism: A practice that involves a practitioner reaching altered states of consciousness in order to perceive and interact with a spirit world and channel these transcendental energies into this world

Sickle: A small to medium sized hand-held, curved blade used for harvesting

Silver branch: A ritual tool used to signify the start of ritual, or to travel between the worlds, as in Celtic mythology

Smudging: To bless an area with a smouldering bundle of herbs, traditionally from the Native American religions using sage

Staff: Druid tool used to direct energy, hold power or used as an aid to walking or hiking. Represents the World Tree or the sacred bile of Irish mythology.

Tech-an-alais: Celtic sweat lodge

Tumuli: Ancient burial mound found dotted all across Europe

Wheel of the Year: An annual cycle of seasonal festivals, observed by many modern Pagans. It consists of either four or eight festivals: either the solstices and equinoxes, known as the 'quarter days', or the four midpoints between, known as the 'cross quarter days'.

Bibliography

Cowan, T. (1993) *Fire in the Head: Shamanism and the Celtic Spirit*, Harper One

Forest, D. (2013) *The Druid Shaman: Exploring the Celtic Otherworld*, Moon Books

Green, M. J. (1997) *Exploring the World of the Druids*, Thames and Hudson

Kirkey, J. (2010) *The Salmon in the Spring: The Ecology of Celtic Spirituality*, Hiraeth Press

Matthews, C. & Matthews, J. (1994) *Encyclopaedia of Celtic Wisdom: A Celtic Shaman's Sourcebook*, Element

Matthews, J. (2001) *The Celtic Shaman: A Practical Guide*, Rider

Restall Orr, E. (2000) *Ritual: A Guide to Life, Love and Inspiration*, Thorsons

Talboys, G.K. (2011) *The Druid Way Made Easy*, O Books

Talboys, G.K. (2006) *Way of the Druid: Rebirth of an Ancient Religion*, O-Books

Talboys, G.K & White, J. (2002) *The Path Through the Forest: A Druid Guidebook*, Grey House in the Woods

van der Hoeven, J. (2014) *The Awen Alone: Walking the Path of the Solitary Druid*, Moon Books

van der Hoeven, J. (2014) *Dancing with Nemetona: A Druid's Exploration of Sanctuary and Sacred Space*, Moon Books

Further Reading

Billington, P. (2011) *The Path of Druidry: Walking the Ancient Green Way*, Llewellyn

Carr-Gomm, P. (2002) *Druid Mysteries: Ancient Wisdom for the 21st Century*, Rider

Carr-Gomm, P. (2002) *In the Grove of the Druids: The Druid Teachings of Ross Nichols*, Watkins Publishing

Freeman, M. (2000) *Kindling the Celtic Spirit*, Harper Collins

Hopman, E. E. (1995) *A Druid's Herbal for the Sacred Earth Year*, Inner Traditions Bear and Company

Hopman, E. E. (2008) *A Druid's Herbal of Sacred Tree Medicine*, Inner Traditions International

Hopman, E. E (2012) *Priestess of the Fire Temple: A Druid's Journey*, Llewellyn

Hopman, E. E. (2008) *Priestess of the Forest: A Druid Novel*, Llewellyn

Hopman, E. E (2010) *The Druid Isle*, Llewellyn

Hutton, R. (2011) *Blood and Mistletoe: The History of the Druids in Britain*, Yale University Press

MacEowan, F. H. (2002) *The Mist-filled Path: Celtic Wisdom for Exiles, Wanderers and Seekers*, New World Library

Matthews, C. (2004) *Celtic Devotional: Daily Prayers and Blessings*, Gill & Macmillan

Restall Orr, E. (1998) *Principles of Druidry*, Thorsons

Restall Orr, E. (2004) *Living Druidry: Magical Spirituality for the Wild Soul London*, Piatkus Books

Restall Orr, E. (2014) *Spirits of the Sacred Grove: The World of a Druid Priestess*, Moon Books Classics

Treadwell, C. (2012) *A Druid's Tale*, John Hunt Publishing

Internet Resources

Druid College UK: www.uk.druidcollege.org
The British Druid Order: www.druidry.co.uk
The Druid Network: www.druidnetwork.org
The Order of Bards, Ovates and Druids: www.druidry.org
The Order of White Oak (Ord na Darach Gile):
  www.whiteoakdruids.org

Other Books by the Author

The Awen Alone: Walking the Path of the Solitary Druid

Druidry is a wonderful, spiritually fulfilling life path. Through the magic of Druidry, we build deep and abiding relationships with the natural world around us, and through our connection to the natural environment we walk a path of truth, honour and service. Throughout the ages, people have withdrawn from the world in order to connect more fully with it. This book is an introductory guide for those who wish to walk the Druid path alone, for however long a time. It is about exploration and connection with the natural world, and finding our place within it. It covers the basics of Druidry and how, when applied to everyday life, it enriches it with a sense of beauty, magic and mystery. This book is for those people who feel called to seek their own path, to use their wit and intelligence, compassion and honour to create their own tradition within Druidry.

Zen Druidry: Living a Natural Life with Full Awareness

Taking both Zen and Druidry and integrating them into your life can be a wonderful and ongoing process of discovery, not only of the self, but also of the entire world around you. Looking at ourselves and at the natural world, we realise that everything is in constant flux: like waves on the ocean, they are all united as a body of water. Even after the wave crashes upon the shore, the ocean is still there, the wave is still there; it has merely changed its form. The aim of this text is an introduction to how Zen teachings and Druidry can combine, creating a peaceful life path that is completely and utterly dedicated to the here and now, to the earth and her rhythms, and to the flow that is life itself.

Dancing With Nemetona: A Druid's Exploration of Sanctuary and Sacred Space

Nemetona is an ancient goddess whose song is heard deep within the earth and also deep within the human soul. She is the Lady of Sanctuary, of Sacred Groves and Sacred Spaces. She is present within the home, within our sacred groves, our rites and in all the spaces that we hold dear to our hearts. She also lies within, allowing us to feel at ease wherever we are in the world through her energy of holding and of transformation. She is the energy of sacred space, where we can stretch out our souls and truly come alive, filled with the magic of potential. Rediscover this ancient goddess and dance with a Druid to the songs of Nemetona. Learn how to reconnect with this goddess in ritual, songs, chants, meditation and more.

Zen for Druids: A Further Guide to Integration, Compassion and Harmony with Nature

The teachings of Zen Buddhism combined with the earth-based tradition of Druidry can create a holistic way of life that is deeply integrated with the seasons, the environment and the present moment. In soul-deep relationship we can use the techniques and wisdom from both traditions to find balance and harmony within our own lives. In this follow-up work to the Pagan Portals *Zen Druidry* by the same author, we explore the concepts of the Dharma (the Buddha's teachings) and how they relate to the wisdom of the Druid tradition. We also look at the Wheel of the Year in modern Druidry with regards to the Dharma, incorporating the teachings into every seasonal festival in an all-encompassing celebration of nature. We explore meditation, mindfulness, animism and integration with nature, learning how to find sustainable relationship in the work that we do, opening our souls to the here and now and seeing the beauty and wonder that enchants our lives in every waking moment. Step into a new life, fully awake and aware to the beauty of the natural world.

About the Author

Joanna van der Hoeven was born in Quebec, Canada. She moved to the UK in 1998, where she now lives with her husband in a small village in Suffolk, near the coast of the North Sea.

Joanna is a Druid, author, teacher, poet, singer and dancer. She has studied with Emma Restall Orr and the Order of Bards, Ovates and Druids. She has a BA Hons English Language and Literature degree. She is currently the media co-ordinator for The Druid Network also works as a Druid priestess for her community. She is also co-founder and tutor at Druid College UK. She gives talks and workshops regularly on meditation, Druidry, Zen Buddhism and more.

For more information, please visit:

www.joannavanderhoeven.com

MOON
BOOKS

Moon Books

PAGANISM & SHAMANISM

What is Paganism? A religion, a spirituality, an alternative belief system, nature worship? You can find support for all these definitions (and many more) in dictionaries, encyclopaedias, and text books of religion, but subscribe to any one and the truth will evade you. Above all Paganism is a creative pursuit, an encounter with reality, an exploration of meaning and an expression of the soul. Druids, Heathens, Wiccans and others, all contribute their insights and literary riches to the Pagan tradition. Moon Books invites you to begin or to deepen your own encounter, right here, right now. If you have enjoyed this book, why not tell other readers by posting a review on your preferred book site.

We think you will also enjoy...

Dancing with Nemetona
Joanna van der Hoeven
An in-depth look at a little-known Goddess who can help bring
peace and sanctuary into your life

*Joanna's book welcomes us into Nemetona's sanctuary that we might
know her more intimately*
Philip Carr-Gomm

978-1-78279-327-4 (paperback)
978-1-78279-326-7 (e-book)

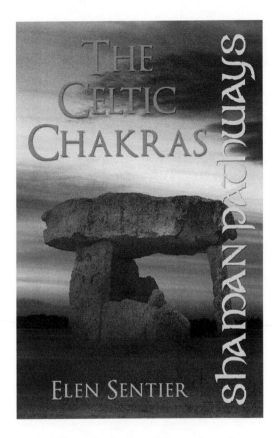

Druid Shaman, Danu Forest

A practical guide to Celtic shamanism with exercises and
techniques as well as traditional lore for exploring the Celtic
Otherworld

A sound, practical introduction to a complex and wide-ranging subject
Philip Shallcrass

978-1-78099-615-8 (paperback)
978-1-78099-616-5 (e-book)

Kitchen Witchcraft, Rachel Patterson

Take a glimpse at the workings of a Kitchen Witch and share in the crafts

A wonderful little book which will get anyone started on Kitchen Witchery. Informative, and easy to follow
Janet Farrar & Gavin Bone

978-1-78099-843-5 (paperback)
978-1-78099-842-8 (e-book)

Moon Magic, Rachel Patterson

An introduction to working with the phases of the Moon

...a delightful treasury of lore and spiritual musings that should be essential to any planetary magic-worker's reading list.
David Salisbury

978-1-78279-281-9 (paperback)
978-1-78279-282-6 (e-book)

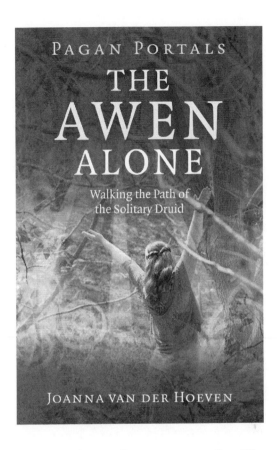

The Awen Alone, Joanna van der Hoeven

An introductory guide for the solitary Druid

Joanna's voice carries the impact and knowledge of the ancestors,
combined with the wisdom of contemporary understanding.
Cat Treadwell

978-1-78279-547-6 (paperback)
978-1-78279-546-9 (e-book)

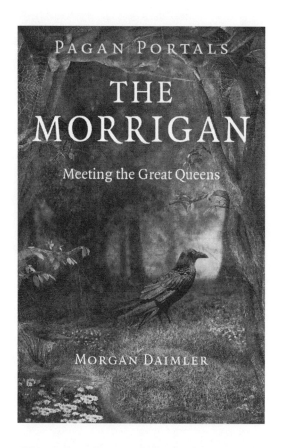

The Morrigan, Morgan Daimler

On shadowed wings and in raven's call, meet the ancient Irish
Goddess of war, battle, prophecy, death, sovereignty, and magic

*...a well-researched and heartfelt guide to the Morrigan from a fellow
devotee and priestess*
Stephanie Woodfield

978-1-78279-833-0 (paperback)
978-1-78279-834-7 (e-book)